D1711013

LPI Linux Certification: Basic Level 1

By Terry Sanchez- Clark

LPI Linux Certification: Basic Level 1

ISBN: 1-933804-71-8

Edited By: Jamie Fisher

Printed in the United States of America

Please visit our website at www.itcookbook.com

Table of Contents

Introduction

Linux is a form of the UNIX operating system. Though originally UNIX was used mainly by engineers and scientists and thus was not well known to the general public. A lot of what you take for granted on computer systems today began in UNIX. A notable example is the Internet, the first major operating system to implement the TCP/IP protocol at the heart of the Internet was UNIX and that led to the general acceptance of the protocol.

In the early 1990s, computer science student Linus Torvalds decided to write his own version of UNIX, which he called Linux. Other "homegrown" versions of UNIX had been written, such as MINIX, but what distinguished Linux was the scale of worldwide participation involved. Torvalds innocently put a message on the Internet asking if anyone wanted to help and he got an avalanche of responses. There are a several reasons why Linux is the mainstream today. First, it became known as a very reliable, stable operating system, with one result being that Linux has become a major platform for large corporate Web servers. Another reason is that it, and the software associated with it developed elsewhere, is free. Many companies have found that it is cheaper to run Linux on their PCs, both for this reason and because of reduced maintenance costs.

Linux has historically been used mainly as a server operating system, but its low cost, flexibility, and UNIX background make it suitable for a wide range of applications. Linux is the cornerstone of the "LAMP" server-software combination (Linux, Apache, MySQL, Perl/PHP/Python) which has achieved popularity among developers, and which is one of the more common platforms for website hosting.

Due to its low cost and its high configurability, Linux is often used in embedded systems such as television set-top boxes, mobile phones, and handheld devices. Linux has become a major competitor to the proprietary Symbian OS found in many mobile phones, and it is an alternative to the dominant Windows CE and Palm OS operating systems on handheld devices. The popular TiVo digital video recorder uses a customized version of Linux. Several network firewall and router standalone products, including several from Linksys, use Linux internally, using its advanced firewalling and routing capabilities. Linux is increasingly common as an operating system for supercomputers. In the November 2005 TOP500 list of supercomputers, the two fastest supercomputers in the world ran Linux. Of the 500 systems, 371 (74.2%) ran some version of Linux, including seven of the top ten.

Clusters of Linux machines are used in the creation of movies such as "Titanic", "Shrek" and others. In post offices, they are the nerve centers that route mail and in large search engine, clusters are used to perform internet searches. These are only a few of the thousands of heavy-duty jobs that Linux is performing day-to-day across the world.

The Sony PlayStation 3 video game console, scheduled to be released in November 2006, will run Linux by default. Sony has previously released a PS2 Linux do-it-yourself kit for their PlayStation 2 video game console. Game developers like Atari and id Software have released titles to the Linux desktop. Linux Game Publishing also produces games for Linux, licensing and porting them from their Windows source code. The One Laptop per Child project, which aims to provide computing devices to all children in developing nations, uses Linux as the devices' operating system.

It is also worth to note that modern Linux not only runs on workstations, mid- and high-end servers, but also on "gadgets" like PDA's, mobiles, a shipload of embedded applications and even on experimental wristwatches. This makes Linux the only operating system in the world covering such a wide range of hardware.

Linux is an open source operating system which is free as in freedom, so that the source code is available for anybody to view, distribute, use, and edit. Everybody is allowed to edit the program to suit his or her own needs, or give it away. This is in contrast to Windows, where the source code can be edited and reviewed only by Microsoft employees and people who agree to sign a non-disclosure agreement. Linux advocates claim that their openness means that code can be reviewed by many people, who can submit bug fixes or new features.

At first a computer running Minix was necessary in order to configure and install Linux. Initial versions of Linux also required another operating system to be present in order to boot from a hard disk, but soon there were independent boot loaders such as LILO. The Linux system quickly surpassed Minix in functionality; Torvalds and other early Linux kernel developers adapted their work for the GNU components and user-space programs to create a complete, fully functional, and free operating system.

Today, Torvalds continues to direct the development of the kernel, while other subsystems such as the GNU components continue to be developed separately (Linux kernel development is not part of the GNU Project). Other groups and companies combine and distribute these components with additional application software in the form of Linux distributions.

Linux is predominantly used as part of a Linux distribution (commonly called a "distro"). These are compiled by individuals, loose-knit teams, and commercial and volunteer organizations. They commonly include additional system and application software, an installer system to ease initial system setup, and integrated management of software installation and upgrading. Distributions are created for many different purposes, including computer architecture support, localization to a specific region or language, real-time applications, and embedded systems, and many deliberately include only free software. Currently, over three hundred distributions are actively developed, with about a dozen distributions being most popular for general-purpose use.

A typical general-purpose distribution includes the Linux kernel, some GNU libraries and tools, command-line shells, the graphical X Window System and an accompanying desktop environment such as KDE or GNOME, together with thousands of application software packages, from office suites to compilers, text editors, and scientific tools
Linux is a combination of several different technologies. The Linux Kernel was started in 1991 (based on earlier kernels), while the X Window System, which provides graphics in Linux, and the GNU project, which is a set of command-line based tools similar to MS-DOS, were both started in 1984.

There are several good reasons for you to use Linux:

As mentioned, Linux is becoming one of the "hottest" software systems. Virtually all of the major companies—IBM, HP, Sun Microsystems, etc.—are promoting it and Linux is a leading corporate choice for Web servers. Linux is the main operating system used.

Linux is also starting to make inroads in large desktop markets, such as businesses, schools and so on, due to its high reliability, lower rate of infection by viruses and the like, and its low cost.

The Linux community shares. That means that people online are much more willing to help you and more open source software is available. If you are a university computer science student, there are some very important additional advantages:

Many CS courses make specific use of UNIX, and thus their work cannot be done on Windows platforms. Since it is a full UNIX system, Linux allows students to do their homework in the comfort of their own homes.

In installing and using Linux, students learn many practical things about computers which they do not learn in coursework. This practical experience can also help you in job interviews, both for permanent jobs after graduation and for summer jobs and co-ops during your college years. Even if the job you interview for does not involve UNIX, you will definitely impress the interviewer if, for example, you discuss various things you have done to use and customize your Linux system.

Chapter I: Linux Basics

Question 01: Shells

What is a shell?

A: A shell can best be described as a language to communicate with a computer. Most users operate with the point-and-click language of the desktop but the computer is leading the conversation in this kind of language. The user has the passive role of picking tasks from the choice presented by the computer. It is very difficult for a programmer to include all options and possible uses of a command in the Graphical User Interface (GUI) format. Thus, GUIs are almost always less capable than the command or commands that form the backend.

Shell is an advanced way of communicating with the system because it allows for two-way conversation. Interactions in the communication are equal so that new ideas can be tested. The shell allows the user to handle a system in a very flexible way and allows for task automation.

When you mess around in the Linux command line, there's always a program called shell running. When you type commands, it's the shell that reads the commands from your keyboard, processes them and finally gives them to the operating system. There are many different shell programs available but on most Linux systems, bash (Bourne Again Shell) is the default shell. When you start a shell on your Linux system, it's most likely bash.

Question 02: Virtual Terminal and Terminal Emulator

I'm in the X Window System (the GUI) right now. How do I get to the Command Line Interfaces (CLI)?

A: You can start playing with the CLI by switching to another virtual terminal or you can start a terminal emulator.

A terminal emulator is a program that opens up a window and then runs a shell in that window. Start a terminal emulator like any other X program, so it means that you can have a command line while you're still safely in the GUI. Now browse the programs menu that you normally use for launching programs and look for applications that seem like a terminal emulator (xterm, rxvt, gnome-terminal, konsole, kvt, eterm, etc...). You can launch as many of them as you want and try all of them. They all basically do the same thing; it lets you use the shell. The different terminal emulators run the same shell program bash, in each of them.

Another way of getting to the CLI is to switch to another virtual terminal while the X Window System is still running. By default, Linux usually has six virtual terminals and the seventh one is where X is running. You can switch the virtual terminals by pressing Ctrl+Alt and the function key with the number of the desired terminal. Pressing Ctrl+Alt+F1 takes you to the first virtual terminal, Ctrl+Alt+F2 takes you to the second virtual terminal and so on.

When you're in the virtual terminals, you're not in the GUI (X Window System) anymore but in the CLI. The GUI is still running in the seventh virtual terminal so you can just switch back there normally with Ctrl+Alt+F7.

When the terminal displays the login: prompt, you can now type in your user name and log in normally in the terminal. Maybe doing things in X with a terminal emulator would be easier at first but it doesn't matter because the result is the same: you have a bash prompt in front of you. The prompt will wait for you to type a command or a name of a program. For example, try typing "ls". As you can see from the output, the command "ls" list the contents of your current directory. All the commands in Linux are little programs themselves and you can run the programs by typing their name.

Question 03: Linux directory structure

How is the Linux file system structured?

A: The following are some list of directories that will show you the most interesting places in your file system.

< / >: The root directory is the starting point of your directory structure and it is where the Linux system begins. Every other file and directory on your system is under the root directory. Usually the root directory contains only subdirectories and it is not advisable to store single files directly under root.

< /boot >: This is where Linux keeps information that it needs when booting up. If you list the contents of /boot, you'll see a file called vmlinuz - that's the kernel.

< /etc >: This is the configuration files for the Linux system. Most of these files are text files and can be edited manually. Here are some interesting contents of this directory:

- /etc/inittab: A text file that describes what processes are started at system bootup and during normal operation. Here you can determine if you want the X Window System to start automatically at bootup and configure what happens when a user presses Ctrl+Alt+Del.

- /etc/fstab: This file contains descriptive information about the various file systems and their mount points, like floppies, cdroms, etc.

- /etc/passwd: A file that contains various pieces of information for each user account. This is where the users are defined.

< /bin, /usr/bin >: These two directories contain a lot of programs for the system. The /bin directory contains the most important programs that the system needs to operate, such as the shells, ls, grep, and other essential things. /usr/bin in turn contains applications for the system's users.

- < /sbin, /usr/sbin >: Most system administration programs are stored in these directories. In many cases you must run these programs as the root user.

- < /usr >: This directory contains user applications and a variety of other things for them, like their source codes, pictures, docs, or config files they use. /usr is the largest directory on a Linux system and some people like to have it on a separate partition. Here are some contents of the /usr:

  1. /usr/doc: Documentation for the user apps in many files formats.
  2. /usr/share: Config files and graphics for many user apps.
  3. /usr/src: Source code files for the system's software including the Linux kernel.
  4. /usr/include: Header files for the C compiler. The header files define structures and constants that are needed for building most standard programs. A subdirectory under /usr/include contains headers for the C++ compiler.
  5. /usr/X11R6: The subdirectories under /usr/X11R6 may contain some X binaries themselves as well as documentation, header files, config files, icons, sounds and things related to the graphical programs.
  6. < /usr/local >: This is where you install apps and other files for use on the local machine. If you find interesting apps that aren't officially a part of your distro, you should install them in /usr/local. For example, if the app would normally go to /usr/bin but it isn't a part of your distro, you should install it in /usr/local/bin instead. Keep your own programs away from the programs that are included in your distro, to confusion and keep things in order.

< /lib >: The shared libraries for programs that are dynamically linked.

< /home >: This is where users keep their personal files. Every user has their own directory under /home, and usually it's the

only place where normal users are allowed to write files. You can configure a Linux system so that normal users can't even list the contents of other users' home directories.

< /root >: The superuser's (root's) home directory. You should not confuse this with the root directory (/) of a Linux system.

< /var >: This directory contains variable data that changes constantly when the system is running. Some interesting subdirectories:

1. /var/log: A directory that contains system log files. These are updated when the system runs and if something in your system suddenly goes wrong, the log files may contain some info about the situation.
2. /var/mail: Incoming and outgoing mail is stored in this directory.
3. /var/spool: This directory holds files that are queued for some process like printing.

< /tmp >: Programs can write their temporary files here.

< /dev >: The devices that are available to a Linux system. In Linux, devices are treated like files and you can read and write devices like they were files.

< /mnt >: This directory is used for mount points. The different physical storage devices must be attached to some directory in the file system tree before they can be accessed. This attaching is called mounting and the directory where the device is attached is called the mount point. The /mnt directory contains mount points for different devices, like /mnt/floppy for the floppy drive, /mnt/cdrom for the CD-ROM and so on. However, you're not forced to use the /mnt directory for this purpose, you can use whatever directory you wish. Actually in some distros, like Debian and SUSE, the default is to use /floppy and /cdrom as mount points instead of directories under /mnt.

< /proc >: This is a special directory. Actually /proc is just a virtual directory because it doesn't exist at all. It contains some info about the kernel itself. There's a bunch of numbered entries that correspond to all processes running on the system and there

are also named entries that permit access to the current configuration of the system. Many of these entries can be viewed.

< /lost found >: This is where Linux keeps the files that it restores after a system crash or when a partition hasn't been uncounted before a system shutdown. This way you can recover files that would otherwise have been lost.

Question 04: Command-line history

What are functions of the history command?

A: The history command can be used to list Bash's logs of the commands you have typed. This log is called the "history". To access it type:

The "history n" will only list the last n commands. You can type "history" (without options) to see the entire history list.

You can also type "!n" to execute command number n. Use "!!" to execute the last command you typed.

The "!-n" will execute the command n times before (ie. !-1 is equivalent to !!).

The "!string" will execute the last command starting with that string and "!?string?" will execute the last command containing the word "string".

For example:

!cd will re-run the command that you last typed starting with "cd".

" commandName !*" will execute the "commandName" with any arguments you used on your last command. This maybe useful if you make a spelling mistake, for example. If you typed: emasc /home/fred/mywork.java /tmp/testme.java

In an attempt to execute emacs on the above two files this will obviously fail. So what you can do is type:

emacs !* will execute emacs with the arguments that you last typed on the command line. In other words this is equivalent to typing:

```
emacs /home/fred/mywork.java /tmp/testme.java
```

To search through the Command History (CTRL-R) : sse the CTRL-R key to perform a "reverse-i-search". For example, if you wanted to use the command you used the last time you used snort, you would type: CTRL-R then type "snort".

What you will see in the console window is: (reverse-i-search)`':

After you have typed what you are looking for, use the CTRL-R key combination to scroll backward through the history.

Use CTRL-R repeatedly to find every reference to the string you have entered. Once you've found the command you're looking for, use [Enter] to execute it.

Alternatively, using the right or left arrow keys will place the command on an actual command line so you can edit it.

Question 05: Linux keyboard shortcuts

In MS Windows, there are a lot of keyboard shortcuts that is used to make life easier for users.

Does Linux have this also?

A: There are several keyboard shortcuts in Linux and here are some of them. Some X Window System shortcuts are also included:

VIRTUAL TERMINALS:

Ctrl + Alt + F1: Switch to the first virtual terminal. In Linux, you can have several virtual terminals at the same time. The default is 6.

Ctrl + Alt + Fn: Switch to the nth virtual terminal. Because the number of virtual terminals is 6 by default, n = 1...6.

tty: Typing the tty command tells you what virtual terminal you're currently working in.

Ctrl + Alt + F7: Switch to the GUI. If you have X Window System running, it runs in the seventh virtual terminal by default. If X isn't running this terminal is empty.

X WINDOW SYSTEM:

Ctrl + Alt + +: Switch to the next resolution in the X Window System. This works if you've configured more than one resolution for your X server. You must use the + in your numpad.

Ctrl + Alt + -: Switch to the previous X resolution. Use the - in your numpad.

MiddleMouseButton: Paste the highlighted text. You can highlight the text with your left mouse button (or with some other highlighting method, depending on the application you're using) and then press the middle mouse button to paste. This is the traditional way of copying and pasting in the X Window System, but may not work in some X applications.

If you have a two-button mouse, pressing both of the buttons at the same time has the same effect as pressing the middle one. If it doesn't, you must enable 3-mouse-button emulation. This works also in text terminals if you enable the gpm service.

Ctrl + Alt + Backspace: Kill the X server. Use this if X crashes and you can't exit it normally. If you've configured your X Window System to start automatically at boot up, this restarts the server and throws you back to the graphical login screen.

COMMAND LINE INPUT:

Home or Ctrl + a: Moves the cursor to the beginning of the current line.

End or Ctrl + e: Moves the cursor to the end of the current line.

Alt + b: Moves the cursor to the beginning of the current or previous word. Note that while this works in virtual terminals, it may not work in all graphical terminal emulators because many graphical applications already use this as a menu shortcut by default.

Alt + f: Moves the cursor to the end of the next word. Again, like with all shortcuts that use Alt as the modifier, this may not work in all graphical terminal emulators.

Tab: Autocomplete commands and file names. Type the first letter(s) of a command, directory or file name, press Tab and the rest is completed automatically. If there are more commands starting with the same letters, the shell completes as much as it can and beeps. If you then press Tab again, it shows you all the alternatives.

This shortcut is really helpful and saves a lot of typing. It even works at the lilo prompt and in some X applications.

Ctrl + u: Erases the current line.

Ctrl + k: Deletes the line from the position of the cursor to the end of the line.

Ctrl + w: Deletes the word before the cursor.

COMMAND LINE OUTPUT:

Shift + PageUp: Scroll terminal output up.

Shift + PageDown: Scroll terminal output down.

Ctrl + l: The clear command clears all previously executed commands and their output from the current terminal.

reset: If you mess up your terminal, use the reset command. Note that you may not be able to see the command when you're typing it.

COMMAND LINE HISTORY:

history: This gives you a list of the commands you previously executed when you type this command.

ArrowUp or Ctrl + p: Scroll up in the history and edit the previously executed commands.

ArrowDown or Ctrl + n: Scroll down in the history and edit the next commands.

Ctrl + r: This shortcut finds the last command that contained the letters you're typing. For example, if you want to find out the last parameters you gave to the "cp" command, you'll press Ctrl + r and type in "cp".

MISCELLANEOUS COMMAND LINE:

Ctrl + c: Kills the current process.

Ctrl + z: This sends the current process to background. It is useful if you have a program running and you need the terminal for awhile but don't want to exit the program completely. Type the command fg to get the process back.

Ctrl + d: Log out from the current terminal. If you use this in a terminal emulator under X, this usually shuts down the terminal emulator after logging you out.

Ctrl + Alt + Del: Reboot the system. You can change this behavior by editing /etc/inittab if you want the system to shut down instead of rebooting.

Question 06: Same path for all the users

Is there an easy procedure to get the same path for all the users?

A: The most important settings are possible to set in the global shell initialization files for login shells: /etc/csh.login for tcsh and /etc/profile for bash.

Exceptions that do not get the right path from these files are rsh commands, ssh commands, menu items from X window manager that do not explicitly start login shell, commands invoked from inittab, cron jobs, daemons jobs like magic filters started from lprd, WWW CGI scripts, and so on.

If the path is set in /etc/csh.cshrc, the path is right even when rsh or ssh execute command in remote machine with account using tcsh/csh. However, it is not possible to set path if account uses bash/sh.

It is possible to combine the path setting to one file, for example to a file /etc/environment-common. There we write:

```
${EXPORT}PATH${EQ}/bin:/usr/bin:/sbin:/usr/sbin:/usr/
bin/X11:/usr/local/bin:/usr/games:.
```

This can be used from /etc/csh.login (for tcsh and csh)

```
    set EQ=" " set EXPORT="setenv " source
/etc/environment-common
```

And from /etc/profile (for bash, doesn't work for ordinary sh)

```
    EQ='=' EXPORT="export " . /etc/environment-common
```

And from /etc/environment (for XDM)

```
    EQ="=" EXPORT="export " . /etc/environment-common
```
This strategy works mostly but ssh will complain of the lines in /etc/environment (and defined environment variables EQ and EXPORT). And still, rsh commands executed with bash won't get this path.

Question 07: Recover root password

How can I recover the root password on RH Linux AS?

A: If you are using Lilo : Type at lilo: linux 1 and it will let you in Single User Mode.

If you are using Grub: Press e when grub menu shows. There is line which starts with kernel, then highlight that line and type e again and then put -s and press escape and press b to boot your System. This procedure will let you in Single User Mode.

Change your password by passwd command.

Question 08: Init

What is initialization?

A: The term "init" (short for "initialization") is the program on Unix and Unix-like systems which spawns all other processes. It runs as a daemon and typically has PID 1.

The functionality diverged considerably between BSD and System V. The usage on most Linux distributions is compatible with System V, but some distributions, such as Slackware, use a BSD-style and others, such as Gentoo Linux, have their own customized version.

Init is a parent process for all the other processes of the system. Other processes inherit environment of the init process and the path is the init path in the rare case that no other path is set.

The 'init path' is fixed in the source of the init program and it is:
`/usr/local/sbin:/sbin:/bin:/usr/sbin:/usr/bin`

Note that init path does not contain /usr/local/bin.

All the programs that are started from /etc/inittab work in init environment, especially system initialization scripts in /etc/init.d (Debian 1.3).

Everything that is started from system initialization scripts has init environment as default environment. For example, syslogd, kerneld, pppd (when started from startup), gpm and most importantly lpd and inetd have init environment and they do not change it.

A group of programs are started from startup scripts but the PATH environment variable is explicitly set in the startup script. Examples are: atd, sendmail, apache and squid.

There are other programs that are started from boot scripts but they change the path completely. One such example is cron.

Question 09: Change user ID

How do I change user ID?

A: Command "su" sets a new user ID to use. If no user ID is given, root is used.

Usually, su invokes a subshell with a different user ID. With argument '-' (more recent synonyms -l or --login) su invokes shell like login shell. However, it does not use login program to do this but uses another built-in path for login 'simulation' (term used in the source code).

For:

normal users: `/usr/local/bin:/usr/bin:/bin:/usr/bin/X11:`

root user:
`/sbin:/bin:/usr/sbin:/usr/bin:/usr/bin/X11:/usr/local`
`/sbin:/usr/local/bin`

There is a group of commands that make use of super user commands safer. They allow better logging, user-based restrictions and usage of individual passwords. The most widely used is sudo:

```
$ sudo env
```

This command modifies the search path so that the current directory is always the last one but it does not modify PATH environment variable. 'sudo env' and 'env' give the same value for PATH variable. Sudo just adds a couple of environment variables like SUDO_USER.

Question 10: Head and Tail

How does head and tail function?

A: These two commands display the n first/last lines of a file respectively. To see the last ten commands entered:

```
wayne:~> tail -10 .bash_history
locate configure | grep bin
man bash
cd
xawtv &
grep usable /usr/share/dict/words
grep advisable /usr/share/dict/words
info quota
man quota
echo $PATH
frm
```

The command head works similarly. The tail command has a handy feature to continuously show the last n lines of a file that changes all the time.

Question 11: The ps command

How do I get the list of processes currently running?

A: The "ps" command will provide you a list of processes currently running. Use the "ps –ef" command and you will be able to see exactly what is running on your system and kill run-away processes or those that are causing problems.

Another use of the ps command is to see what users are currently doing. Use ps –u user (e.g. jim) will give you a sample output of:

```
user@server:~> ps -u jim

20876 pts/1    00:00:00 bash
20904 pts/2    00:00:00 bash
20951 pts/2    00:00:00 ssh
21012 pts/1    00:00:00 ps
```

From this we can see that the user is doing ps ssh.

COMMAND-LINE OPTIONS:
This version of ps accepts several kinds of options.

Unix98 options may be grouped and must be preceeded by a dash.
BSD options may be grouped and must not be used with a dash.
GNU long options are preceeded by two dashes.

Options of different types may be freely mixed.

Set the I_WANT_A_BROKEN_PS environment variable to force BSD syntax even when options are preceeded by a dash. The PS_PERSONALITY environment variable (described below) provides more detailed control of ps behavior.

SIMPLE PROCESS SELECTION:
Switch	Description
-A	select all processes
-N	negate selection

-a	select all with a tty except session leaders
-d	select all, but omit session leaders
-e	select all processes
T	select all processes on this terminal
a	select all processes on a terminal, including those of other users
g	really all, even group leaders (does nothing w/o SunOS settings)
r	restrict output to running processes
x	select processes without controlling ttys
--deselect	negate selection

PROCESS SELECTION BY LIST:

Switch	Description
-C	select by command name
-G	select by RGID (supports names)
-U	select by RUID (supports names)
-g	select by session leader OR by group name
-p	select by PID
-s	select processes belonging to the sessions given
-t	select by tty
-u	select by effective user ID (supports names)
U	select processes for specified users
p	select by process ID
t	select by tty
--Group	select by real group name or ID
--User	select by real user name or ID
--group	select by effective group name or ID
--pid	select by process ID
--sid	select by session ID
--tty	select by terminal
--user	select by effective user name or ID
-123	implied --sid
123	implied --pid

OUTPUT FORMAT CONTROL:

Switch	Description
-O	is preloaded "-o"
-c	different scheduler info for -l option
-f	does full listing
-j	jobs format
-l	long format
-o	user-defined format

-y	do not show flags; show rss in place of addr
O	is preloaded "o" (overloaded)
X	old Linux i386 register format
j	job control format
l	display long format
o	specify user-defined format
s	display signal format
u	display user-oriented format
v	display virtual memory format
--format	user-defined format

OUTPUT MODIFIERS:

Switch	Description
-H	show process hierarchy (forest)
-m	show all threads
-n	set namelist file
-w	wide output
C	use raw CPU time for %CPU instead of decaying average
N	specify namelist file
O	sorting order (overloaded)
S	include some dead child process data (as a sum with the parent)
c	true command name
e	show environment after the command
f	ASCII-art process hierarchy (forest)
h	do not print header lines (repeat header lines in BSD personality)
m	all threads
n	numeric output for WCHAN and USER
w	wide output
--cols	set screen width
--columns	set screen width
--cumulative	include some dead child process data (as a sum with the parent)
--forest	ASCII art process tree
--html	HTML escaped output
--headers	repeat header lines
--no-headers	print no header line at all
--lines	set screen height
--nul	unjustified output with NULs
--null	unjustified output with NULs
--rows	set screen height

31

--sorts	specify sorting order
--width	set screen width
--zero	unjustified output with NULs

INFORMATION:

Switch	Description
-V	print version
L	list all format specifiers
V	show version info
--help	print help message
--info	print debugging info
--version	print version

Question 12: pstree

What is a pstree? How does it work?

A: A pstree is a UNIX command that shows the running processes as a tree. Its root is either init process or process for given PID. If a user name is specified, all process trees rooted at processes owned by that user are shown. It is used as alternative to ps command.

The command pstree visually merges identical branches by putting them in square brackets and prefixing them with the repetition count, e.g.

```
init-+-getty
     |-getty
     |-getty
     `-getty
```

becomes

```
init---4*[getty]
```

OPTIONS:
-a
   Show command line arguments. If the command line of a process is swapped out, that
   process is shown in parentheses. -a implicitly disables compaction.
-c
   Disable compaction of identical subtrees. By default, subtrees are compacted whenever
   possible.
-G
   Use VT100 line drawing characters.
-h
   Highlight the current process and its ancestors. This is a no-op if the terminal doesn't
   support highlighting or if neither the current process nor any of its ancestors are in the
   subtree being shown.

-H
   Like -h, but highlight the specified process instead. Unlike with
-h, pstree fails when
   using -H if highlighting is not available.
-l
   Display long lines. By default, lines are truncated to the display
width or 132 if output is
   sent to a non-tty or if the display width is unknown.
-n
   Sort processes with the same ancestor by PID instead of by
name. (Numeric sort.)
-p
   Show PIDs. PIDs are shown as decimal numbers in
parentheses after each process
   name. -p implicitly disables compaction.
-u
   Show uid transitions. Whenever the uid of a process differs
from the uid of its parent,
   the new uid is shown in parentheses after the process name.
-U
   Use UTF-8 (Unicode) line drawing characters. Under Linux
1.1-54 and above, UTF-8
   mode is entered on the console with echo -e '\033%8' and left
with echo -e '\033%@'
-V
   Display version information.
-s
   (Flask) Show Security ID (SID) for each process.
-x
   (Flask) Show security context for each process.

Question 13: Standard Input/Output

Many CLI programs use a feature called input/output redirection.

How do they work?

A: The input/output redirection feature of CLI programs allows you to attach or fuse simple commands together in order to construct a more complex command.

STANDARD OUTPUT:

Many Linux commands print their output to screen. For example, cat does this when it lists the contents of a file and makes you see the output on your screen. However, the screen isn't the only place where the commands can print their output because you can redirect the output of several commands to files, devices and even to the input of other commands.

The CLI programs that display their results do so usually by sending the results to standard output or stdout for short. By default, standard output directs its contents to the screen as you can see with the cat command but if you want to direct the output to somewhere else, you can use the > character, e.g. :

```
$ ls > dir_listing.txt
```

The above redirects the output of the ls command to a file called dir_listing.txt. You won't see any results of ls on your screen since the output is redirected to a file.

Each time you repeat $ ls > dir_listing.txt command, the file dir_listing.txt is overwritten with the results of the ls command. If you want to append the new results to the file instead of rewriting it, you can use >> instead:

```
$ ls >> dir_listing.txt
```

The new output of ls is added at the end of the dir_listing.txt file instead of overwriting the file each time you repeat $ ls >> dir_listing.txt command.

The following adds the contents of File1 at the end of File8:

```
$ cat File1 >> File8
```

You can also redirect it to devices using:

```
$ cat sound.wav > /dev/audio
```

Assume that the cat command concatenates a file named sound.wav and the results are sent to a device called /dev/audio. The above command plays the file sound.wav if your sound is properly configured.

STANDARD INPUT:

Many commands accept input from standard input, or stdin for short. By default, standard input reads information from your keyboard and just like standard output, it can be redirected. To give you a clear idea, we can use a little program called tac when experimenting. This program reads standard input and then displays it to you with all the lines reversed. See how tac works when it reads the input from your keyboard. Give the command tac and type a few lines of text, using Enter for starting new lines. Then press Ctrl+D when you're done, tac then displays the text with all the lines reversed.

```
me@puter: ~$ tac
gorgeous me
also you
also you
gorgeous me
me@puter: ~$
```

You can redirect the input so that tac gets it from a file instead of the keyboard. You can do it with the < character, like this:

```
$ tac < list_abc.txt
```

36

The above reads the input from a file called list_abc.txt and sends the results to standard output. Since the output isn't redirected anywhere, it will be displayed on your screen where you see the lines of lines_abc.txt in reverse order.

You can also redirect both a command's input and output:

```
$ tac < list_abc.txt > list_cba.txt
```

The above does the same thing as the previous command, only this time the results aren't displayed on your screen. Since the output is redirected, the results are written to a file called list_cba.txt which then contains the same lines as list_abc.txt but in the reverse order.

Question 14: Pipes

Can I take the output of one program and send it as the input of another one?

A: Yes and it is called piping. Pipes let you use the output of a program as the input of another one. For example, a simple pipe with sed:

```
ls -l | sed -e "s/[aeio]/u/g"
```

What happens here is that the command ls -l is executed and it's output. Instead of being printed, it is sent or piped to the sed program which in turn prints what it has to.

You can use pipes with many commands and one of the most commonly used is grep. It is a program that examines every line of the standard input it gets and searches for a specified pattern of characters. Then it sends to standard output every line that contains those characters.

Assume we have a text file called list.txt and we want to find out what lines of it contain the word "peace". It can be done easily with pipes. List the contents of the file list.txt and send the results to grep, which in turn filters all lines containing the desired word "peace" and displays those lines on your screen:

```
$ cat list.txt | grep peace
```

Like many Linux commands, grep is case sensitive. This means that the above matches only "peace", not "Peace" or "PEACE". With the -i option, the search is case insensitive:

```
$ cat applist.txt | grep -i desktop
```

A pipe is a very useful feature. Once you get more familiar with the CLI and learn more commands then you'll start to appreciate this feature each time you use it.

Question 15: Command substitution

What is a command substitution? How does it function?

A: Command substitution is basically another way to do a pipe. You can use pipes and command substitution interchangeably. Command substitution can be done in two distinct ways.

1.   Simply type: `command_1 ` `command_2 -options``

This will execute "command_2" and its output will become the input to "command_1".

The back-quote key is usually located at the same place as the tilde, above the [Tab] key.

2 .   Or type: `command_1 $(command_2)`

This will execute "command_2" and its output will become the input to "command_1".

You can of course use pipes to perform the same thing. For example, instead of doing:

`less $cat file1.txt file2.txt`

Do: `cat file1.txt file2.txt | less`

This way, you will end up with exactly the same result.

Question 16: Top command

How important is it for an administrator to monitor the performance of their system?

A: One of the most important responsibilities a system administrator is to monitor their systems. If system resources become too low, it can cause a lot of problems. System resources can be taken up by individual users or by services your system may host such as email or web pages. The ability to know what is happening can help determine whether system upgrades are needed or if some services need to be moved to another machine.

The most common of these commands is top. The <command>top</command> provides an ongoing look at processor activity in real time. It displays a listing of the most CPU-intensive tasks on the system, and can provide an interactive interface for manipulating processes. It can sort the tasks by CPU usage, memory usage and runtime and can be better configured than the standard top from the procps suite. Most features can either be selected by an interactive command or by specifying the feature in the personal or system-wide configuration file.

You can modify the output of top while it is running. If you hit an "I", top will no longer display idle processes. Hit i again to see them again. Hitting M will sort by memory usage, S will sort by how long they processes have been running and P will sort by CPU usage again.

In addition to viewing options, you can also modify processes from within the top command. You can use u to view processes owned by a specific user, k to kill processes and r to remise them.

For more in-depth information about processes you can look in the /proc file system. In the /proc file system you will find a series of sub-directories with numeric names. These directories are associated with the processes ids of currently running processes. In each directory you will find a series of files containing information about the process.

Question 17: vi editor

Why should I opt to use vi editor?

A: Despite its age, "vi" is still an important tool today. This is demonstrated by the fact that every UNIX and Linux distribution released over the last twenty years is likely to have a copy installed by default. Since the original release of "vi", many derivatives have been written (such as vim, vile and elvis), with usability and functionality added along the way. Because of this, "vi" is probably one of the most evolved and stable text editors in the world.

Many of the more recent vi clones are also intelligent enough to know about the type of document you are editing, and will help you out by automatically indenting your text (in the case of HTML or C, for example) or by highlighting the syntax to make your work much clearer. In the great Unix tradition, features that bug you or help you can be turned on and off at your preference, and spending a few minutes customizing vi to your liking can save you hours of work in the long run.

The vi editor is a very powerful tool and has a very extensive built-in manual, which you can activate using the help command when the program is started. What makes vi confusing to the beginner is that it can operate in two modes: command mode and insert mode. The editor always starts in command mode. Commands move you through the text, search, replace, mark blocks and perform other editing tasks and some of them switch the editor to insert mode. This means that each key has not one but likely two meanings: it can either represent a command for the editor when in command mode or a character that you want in a text when in insert mode.

Question 18: Basic vi commands

What are the basic vi commands?

A: The "vi" editor is a common editor for UNIX systems in that it makes use of a regular keyboard with an escape key. On the DECstation, the escape key is the F11 key. It therefore works on all UNIX computers. Complete documentation is available by typing
"man vi" at the UNIX prompt.

Starting an Editing Session:

To start vi just type vi at the operating system prompt. You will see a screen with a column of tildes (~) down the left side of the screen. This signifies an empty workspace. To edit a file, just include the filename after it, e.g. vi filename. You will see the text of the file you included. Vi is now in command mode. The most basic command to enter insert mode is 'i' which lets you insert text to the left of the cursor.

In insert mode the characters you type are inserted into your document. You can use the backspace key to delete any typing mistakes you have made on the current input line. The escape key (<esc>) takes you out of insert mode and back to the command mode. If you are ever in doubt about what mode you are in, just press <esc> a few times until vi starts complaining. You will then know that you are in the command mode.

Command mode is where you do everything that isn't done in insert mode. In command mode the same keys that caused letters to appear on your screen in insert mode now represent totally different functions.

Here are some popular commands:

Undo Command:

U - undo the last command.

Screen Commands:

CTL/l - Reprints current screen.
CTL/L - Exposes one more line at top of screen.
CTL/E - Exposes one more line at bottom of screen.
CTL/F - Pages forward one screen.
CTL/B - Pages back one screen.
CTL/D - Pages down half screen.
CTL/U - Pages up half screen.

Cursor Positioning Commands:

j - Moves cursor down one line, same column.
k - Moves cursor up one line, same column.
h - Moves cursor back one character.
l - Moves cursor forward one character.
RET - Moves cursor to beginning of next line.
0 - Moves cursor to beginning of current line.
$ - Moves cursor to end of current line.
SPACE - Moves cursor forward one character.
nG - Moves cursor to beginning of line n. Default is last line of file.
0 - Moves the cursor to the first character of the line.
:n - Moves cursor to beginning of line n.
b - Moves the cursor backward to the beginning of the previous word.
e - Moves the cursor backward to the end of the previous word.
w - Moves the cursor forward to the next word.
/pattern - Moves cursor forward to next occurrence of pattern.
?pattern - Moves cursor backward to next occurrence of pattern.
N - Repeats last / or ? pattern search.

If you try to move somewhere that vi doesn't want to go, e.g. pressing h when the cursor is in the left-most column, your terminal will complain by either beeping or flashing the screen.

Text Insertion Commands:

a - Appends text after cursor. Terminated by escape key.
A - Appends text at the end of the line. Terminated the escape key.
i - Inserts text before cursor. Terminated by the escape key.
I - Inserts text at the beginning of the line. Terminated by the escape key.

o - Opens new line below the current line for text insertion. Terminated by the escape key.
O - Opens new line above the current line for text insertion. Terminated by the escape
    key.
DEL - Overwrites last character during text insertion.
ESC - Stops text insertion. The escape key on the DECstations is the F11 key.

Text Deletion Commands:

x - Deletes current character.
dd - Deletes current line.
dw - Deletes the current word.
d) - Deletes the rest of the current sentence.
D, d$ - Deletes from cursor to end of line.
P - Puts back text from the previous delete.

Changing Commands:

cw - Changes characters of current word until stopped with escape key.
c$ - Changes text up to the end of the line.
C, cc - Changes remaining text on current line until stopped by pressing the escape key.

~ - Changes case of current character.
xp - Transposes current and following characters.
J - Joins current line with next line.
s - Deletes the current character and goes into the insertion mode.
rx - Replaces current character with x.
R - Replaces the following characters until terminated with the escape key.

Cut and Paste Commands:

yy - Puts the current line in a buffer. Does not delete the line from its current position.
p - Places the line in the buffer after the current position of the cursor.

Appending Files into Current File:

:R filename - inserts the file filename where the cursor was before the ``:" was typed.

Exiting vi:

ZZ - Exits vi and saves changes.
:wq - Writes changes to current file and quits edit session.
:q! - Quits edit session (no changes made).

Question 19: Word count

I want to find out the number of bytes and words in my file. How can I do this?

A: Use "wc" (short for word count), this is a command in Unix-like operating systems.
The program reads either standard input or a list of files and generates one or more of the following statistics: number of bytes, number of words, and number of lines (specifically, the number of new line characters). If a list of files is provided, both individual file and total statistics follow.

For example:

```
$ wc ideas.txt excerpt.txt
    40     149     947 ideas.txt
  2294   16638   97724 excerpt.txt
  2334   16787   98671 total
```

The first column shows the number of lines, the second column shows the number of words and the last column is number of characters.

Newer versions of wc can differentiate between byte and character count. This difference arises with Unicode which includes multi-byte characters. The desired behavior is selected with the -c or -m switch.

Description:
Print byte, word, and new line counts for each FILE, and a total line if more than one FILE is specified. With no FILE, or when FILE is -, read standard input.

-c, --bytes
    print the byte counts
-m, --chars
    print the character counts
-l, --lines
    print the newline counts
-L, --max-line-length

print the length of the longest line
-w, --words
    print the word counts
--help
    display this help and exit
--version
    output version information and exit

Question 20: tr

How can I translate and/or delete characters from a standard input?

A: Use tr (abbreviated from translate or transliterate), it is a command in Unix-like operating systems.

When executed, the program reads from the standard input and writes to the standard output. It takes as parameters two sets of characters, and replaces occurrences of the characters in the first set with the corresponding elements from the other set. The following inputs, for instance, shift the input letters of the alphabet back by one character.

```
$ echo "ibm 9000" >computer.txt
$ tr a-z za-y <computer.txt
hal 9000
```

Description:

-c, --complement
    first complement SET1
-d, --delete
    delete characters in SET1, do not translate
-s, --squeeze-repeats
    replace each input sequence of a repeated character that is listed in SET1 with a
    single occurrence of that character
-t, --truncate-set1
    first truncate SET1 to length of SET2
--help
    display this help and exit
--version
    output version information and exit

SETs are specified as strings of characters. Most represent themselves. Interpreted sequences are:

\NNN

character with octal value NNN (1 to 3 octal digits)

\\

backslash

\a

audible BEL

\b

backspace

\f

form feed

\n

new line

\r

return

\t

horizontal tab

\v

vertical tab

CHAR1-CHAR2

all characters from CHAR1 to CHAR2 in ascending order

[CHAR*]

in SET2, copies of CHAR until length of SET1

[CHAR*REPEAT]

REPEAT copies of CHAR, REPEAT octal if starting with 0

[:alnum:]

all letters and digits

[:alpha:]

all letters

[:blank:]

all horizontal whitespace

[:cntrl:]

all control characters

[:digit:]

all digits

[:graph:]

all printable characters, not including space

[:lower:]

all lower case letters

[:print:]

all printable characters, including space

[:punct:]

all punctuation characters

[:space:]

all horizontal or vertical whitespace

[:upper:]
    all upper case letters
[:xdigit:]
    all hexadecimal digits
[=CHAR=]
    all characters which are equivalent to CHAR

Translation occurs if -d is not given and both SET1 and SET2 appear. -t may be used only when translating. SET2 is extended to length of SET1 by repeating its last character as necessary. Excess characters of SET2 are ignored. Only [:lower:] and [:upper:] are guaranteed to expand in ascending order; used in SET2 while translating, they may only be used in pairs to specify case conversion. -s uses SET1 if not translating nor deleting; else squeezing uses SET2 and occurs after translation or deletion.

Question 21: nice

Is there a way to control or facilitate processes executing quickly so that the processes execute slowly so as not to interfere with other system activities?

A: UNIX processes have an associated system nice value which is used by the kernel to determine when it should be scheduled to run. This value can be increased to facilitate processes executing quickly or decreased so that the processes execute slowly and thus do not interfere with other system activities.

SYNOPSIS:
```
nice [OPTION] [COMMAND [ARG]...]
```

DESCRIPTION:

Run COMMAND with an adjusted scheduling priority. With no COMMAND, print the current scheduling priority. ADJUST is 10 by default. Range goes from -20 (highest priority) to 19 (lowest).

-n, --adjustment=ADJUST
    increment priority by ADJUST first
--help
    display this help and exit
--version
    output version information and exit

Question 22: join

I want to merge the lines of two sorted files based on the presence of a common field.

How do I accomplish that?

A: The command join is Unix-like operating system that merges the lines of two sorted text files based on the presence of a common field. It is a sort of implementation of the join operator used in relational databases but operating on text files.

The join command takes as input two text files and a number of options. If no command-line argument is given, this command looks for a pair of lines from the two files having the same first field (a sequence of characters that are different from space), and outputs a line composed of the first field followed by the rest of the two lines.

The program arguments specify which character to be used in place of space to separate the fields of the line, which field to use when looking for matching lines, and whether to output lines that do not match. The output can be stored to another file rather than printing using redirection.

SYNOPSIS:
```
join [OPTION]... FILE1 FILE2
```

DESCRIPTION:
For each pair of input lines with identical join fields, write a line to standard output. The default join field is the first, delimited by whitespace. When FILE1 or FILE2 (not both) is -, read standard input.

-a SIDE
     print unpairable lines coming from file SIDE
-e EMPTY
     replace missing input fields with EMPTY
-i, --ignore-case
     ignore differences in case when comparing fields
-j FIELD

    (obsolescent) equivalent to `-1 FIELD -2 FIELD'
-j1 FIELD
    (obsolescent) equivalent to `-1 FIELD'
-j2 FIELD
    (obsolescent) equivalent to `-2 FIELD'
-o FORMAT
    obey FORMAT while constructing output line
-t CHAR
    use CHAR as input and output field separator
-v SIDE
    like -a SIDE, but suppress joined output lines
-1 FIELD
    join on this FIELD of file 1
-2 FIELD
    join on this FIELD of file 2
--help
    display this help and exit
--version
    output version information and exit

Unless -t CHAR is given, leading blanks separate fields and are ignored, else fields are separated by CHAR. Any FIELD is a field number counted from 1. FORMAT is one or more comma or blank separated specifications, each being `SIDE.FIELD' or `o'. Default FORMAT outputs the join field, the remaining fields from FILE1, the remaining fields from FILE2, all separated by CHAR.

As an example, the two following files list the known fathers and the mothers of some people:

wayne nico
terry solo

solo krisha
wayne kristel

The join of these two files (with no argument) would produce:

wayne nico kristel

Indeed, only "wayne" is common as a first word of both files.

Question 23: Xargs

What is xargs?

A: The command "xargs" reads arguments from the standard input, delimited by blanks (which can be protected with double or single quotes or a backslash) or newlines, and executes the command (default is /bin/echo) one or more times with any initial-arguments followed by arguments read from standard input. Blank lines on the standard input are ignored. The command xargs exits with the following status:

0   if it succeeds
123 if any invocation of the command exited with status 1-125
124 if the command exited with status 255
125 if the command is killed by a signal
126 if the command cannot be run
127 if the command is not found
1   if some other error occurred.

Options:

--null, -0
    Input filenames are terminated by a null character instead of by whitespace, and the
    quotes and backslash are not special (every character is taken literally). Disables the
    end of file string, which is treated like any other argument. Useful when arguments
    might contain white space, quote marks, or backslashes. The GNU find -print0 option
    produces input suitable for this mode.

--eof[=eof-str], -e[eof-str]
    Set the end of file string to eof-str. If the end of file string occurs as a line of input, the
    rest of the input is ignored. If eof-str is omitted, there is no end of file string. If this
    option is not given, the end of file string defaults to "_".

--help
Print a summary of the options to xargs and exit.

--replace[=replace-str], -i[replace-str]
Replace occurrences of replace-str in the initial arguments
with names read from
standard input. Also, unquoted blanks do not terminate
arguments. If replace-str is
omitted, it defaults to "{}" (like for `find -exec'). Implies -x and
-l 1.

--max-lines[=max-lines], -l[max-lines]
Use at most max-lines nonblank input lines per command line;
max-lines defaults to 1
if omitted. Trailing blanks cause an input line to be logically
continued on the next
input line. Implies -x.

--max-args=max-args, -n max-args
Use at most max-args arguments per command line. Fewer
than max-args arguments
will be used if the size (see the -s option) is exceeded, unless
the -x option is given, in
which case xargs will exit.

--interactive, -p
Prompt the user about whether to run each command line and
read a line from the
terminal. Run the command line only if the response starts
with `y' or `Y'. Implies -t.

--no-run-if-empty, -r
If the standard input does not contain any nonblanks, do not
run the command.
Normally, the command is run once even if there is no input.

--max-chars=max-chars, -s max-chars
Use at most max-chars characters per command line,
including the command and
initial arguments and the terminating nulls at the ends of the
argument strings. The
default is as large as possible, up to 20k characters.

--verbose, -t
  Print the command line on the standard error output before
  executing it.

--version
  Print the version number of xargs and exit.

--exit, -x
  Exit if the size (see the -s option) is exceeded.

--max-procs=max-procs, -P max-procs
  Run up to max-procs processes at a time; the default is 1. If
  max-procs is 0, xargs will
  run as many processes as possible at a time. Use the -n option
  with -P; otherwise
  chances are that only one exec will be done.

xargs is often used in conjunction with the Unix commands find,
locate and grep.

For example:

1. `* find . -name "*.foo" | xargs grep bar`

In practice does the same as grep bar:

`` `find . -name "*.foo"` ``

This will work even if there are so many files to search that they
will not all fit on a single command line. It searches in all files in
the current directory and its subdirectories which end in .foo for
occurrences of the string bar.

2. `* find . -name "*.foo" -print0 | xargs -0 grep bar`

This does the same thing but uses GNU specific extensions to
find and xargs to separate filenames using the null character; this
will work even if there are whitespace characters, including
newlines, in the filenames.

Question 24: SED

What is SED and how is it used?

A: A Stream Editor (sed) is a simple and powerful computer program used to apply various pre-specified textual transformations to a sequential stream of text data. It reads input files line by line, edits each line according to rules specified in its simple language (sed script) and then outputs the line.

Sed is often thought of as a non-interactive text editor. It differs from conventional text editors in that the processing of the two inputs is inverted. Instead of iterating once through a list of edit commands applying each one to the whole text file in memory, sed iterates once through the text file applying the whole list of edit commands to each line. Because only one line at a time is in memory, sed can process text files with an arbitrarily-large number of lines. Some implementations of sed can only process lines of limited lengths.

Most people use sed first for its substitution features. Sed is often used as a find-and-replace tool.

```
sed 's/Wayne/Nico/g' oldfile >newfile
```

It will replace every occurrence of "Wayne" with the word "Nico", wherever it occurs in the file. The "find" portion is a regular expression ("RE"), which can be a simple word or may contain special characters to allow greater flexibility (for example, to prevent "Wayne" from also matching "Wayneme").

sed can be used to add 8 spaces to the left side of a file, the printing wouldn't begin at the absolute left edge of a piece of paper.

```
    sed 's/^/        /' myfile >newfile    # sed
script
    sed 's/^/        /' myfile | lp        # next sed
script
```

sed could display only one paragraph of a file, beginning at the phrase "once upon a time" and ending at the phrase "happily ever after". The script looked like this:

```
sed -n '/once upon a time/,/happily ever
after/p' myfile
```

Sed's normal behavior is to print (i.e., display or show on screen) the entire file, including the parts that haven't been altered, unless you use the -n switch. The "-n" stands for "no output". This switch is almost always used in conjunction with a 'p' command somewhere, which says to print only the sections of the file that have been specified. The -n switch with the 'p' command allow for parts of a file to be printed (i.e., sent to the console).

Question 25: Job Control

I want to carry out a lengthy task in the background while using
the terminal for another purpose. Is it possible to selectively stop
or suspend the execution of some processes?

A: Most tasks (directory listing, editing files, etc.) can easily be
accomplished by letting the program take control of the terminal
and returning control to the shell when the program exits;
however, sometimes the user will wish to carry out a lengthy task
in the background while using the terminal for another purpose.
Job control is a facility developed to make this possible. It allows
the user to start programs in the background, send programs
into the background, bring background programs into the
foreground, and start and stop running programs. Programs
under the influence of a job control facility are referred to as
jobs.

The shell associates a job with each pipeline. It keeps a table of
currently executing jobs, which may be listed with the jobs
command. When Bash starts a job asynchronously, it prints a
line that looks like:

```
[1]  12345
```

Thus, indicating that this job is job number 1 and that the
process ID of the last process in the pipeline associated with this
job is 12345. All of the processes in a single pipeline are
members of the same job. Bash uses the job abstraction as the
basis for job control.

To facilitate the implementation of the user interface to job
control, the operating system maintains the notion of a current
terminal process group ID. Members of this process group
(processes whose process group ID is equal to the current
terminal process group ID) receive keyboard-generated signals
such as SIGINT. These processes are said to be in the
foreground. Background processes are those whose process
group ID differs from the terminal's; such processes are immune
to keyboard-generated signals. Only foreground processes are
allowed to read from or write to the terminal. Background

processes which attempt to read from (write to) the terminals are sent a SIGTTIN (SIGTTOU) signal by the terminal driver, which, unless caught, suspends the process.

If the operating system on which Bash is running supports job control, Bash contains facilities to use it. Typing the suspend character (typically `^Z', Control-Z) while a process is running causes that process to be stopped and returns control to Bash. Typing the delayed suspend character (typically `^Y', Control-Y) causes the process to be stopped when it attempts to read input from the terminal, and control to be returned to Bash. The user then manipulates the state of this job, using the bg command to continue it in the background, the fg command to continue it in the foreground, or the kill command to kill it. A `^Z' takes effect immediately, and has the additional side effect of causing pending output and type ahead to be discarded.

There are a number of ways to refer to a job in the shell. The character `%' introduces a job name.

Job number n may be referred to as `%n'. The symbols `%%' and `%+' refer to the shell's notion of the current job, which is the last job stopped while it was in the foreground or started in the background. A single `%' (with no accompanying job specification) also refers to the current job. The previous job may be referenced using `%-'. In output pertaining to jobs (e.g., the output of the jobs command), the current job is always flagged with a `+', and the previous job with a `-'.

A job may also be referred to using a prefix of the name used to start it, or using a substring that appears in its command line. For example, `%ab' refers to a stopped ab job. Using `%?ab', on the other hand, refers to any job containing the string `ab' in its command line. If the prefix or substring matches more than one job, Bash reports an error.

Simply naming a job can be used to bring it into the foreground: `%1' is a synonym for `fg %1', bringing job 1 from the background into the foreground. Similarly, `%1 &' resumes job 1 in the background, equivalent to `bg %1'

The shell learns immediately whenever a job changes state. Normally, Bash waits until it is about to print a prompt before reporting changes in a job's status so as to not interrupt any other output. If the `-b' option to the set built-in is enabled, Bash reports such changes immediately. Any trap on SIGCHLD is executed for each child process that exits.

If an attempt to exit Bash is made while jobs are stopped, the shell prints a message warning that there are stopped jobs. The jobs command may then be used to inspect their status. If a second attempt to exit is made without an intervening command, Bash does not print another warning, and the stopped jobs are terminated.

Job Control Built-ins:

bg

```
bg [jobspec ...]
```

Resume each suspended job jobspec in the background, as if it had been started with `&'. If jobspec is not supplied, the current job is used. The return status is zero unless it is run when job control is not enabled, or, when run with job control enabled, any jobspec was not found or specifies a job that was started without job control.

fg

```
fg [jobspec]
```

Resume the job jobspec in the foreground and make it the current job. If jobspec is not supplied, the current job is used. The return status is that of the command placed into the foreground, or non-zero if run when job control is disabled or, when run with job control enabled, jobspec does not specify a valid job or jobspec specifies a job that was started without job control.

jobs

```
jobs [-lnprs] [jobspec]
jobs -x command [arguments]
```

The first form lists the active jobs. The options have the following meanings:

-l

List process IDs in addition to the normal information.

-n
   Display information only about jobs that have changed status since the user was last
      notified of their status.

-p
   List only the process ID of the job's process group leader.

-r
   Restrict output to running jobs.

-s
   Restrict output to stopped jobs.

If jobspec is given, output is restricted to information about that job. If jobspec is not
supplied, the status of all jobs is listed.

If the `-x' option is supplied, jobs replaces any jobspec found in command or
arguments with the corresponding process group ID and execute command, passing it
arguments, returning its exit status.

```
kill
      kill [-s sigspec] [-n signum] [-sigspec] jobspec
or pid
      kill -l [exit_status]
```

Send a signal specified by sigspec or signum to the process named by job specification jobspec or process ID pid. sigspec is either a case-insensitive signal name such as SIGINT (with or without the SIG prefix) or a signal number; signum is a signal number. If sigspec and signum are not present, SIGTERM is used. The `-l' option lists the signal names. If any arguments are supplied when `-l' is given, the names of the signals corresponding to the arguments are listed, and the return status is zero. exit_status is a number specifying a signal number or the exit status of a process terminated by a signal. The return status is zero if at least one signal was successfully sent, or non-zero if an error occurs or an invalid option is encountered.

wait

```
wait [jobspec or pid ...]
```

Wait until the child process specified by each process ID pid or job specification jobspec exits and return the exit status of the last command waited for. If a job spec is given, all processes in the job are waited for. If no arguments are given, all currently active child processes are waited for, and the return status is zero. If neither jobspec nor pid specifies an active child process of the shell, the return status is 127.

disown

```
disown [-ar] [-h] [jobspec ...]
```

Without options, each jobspec is removed from the table of active jobs. If the `-h' option is given, the job is not removed from the table, but is marked so that SIGHUP is not sent to the job if the shell receives a SIGHUP. If jobspec is not present, and neither the `-a' nor `-r' option is supplied, the current job is used. If no jobspec is supplied, the `-a' option means to remove or mark all jobs; the `-r' option without a jobspec argument restricts operation to running jobs.

suspend

```
suspend [-f]
```

Suspend the execution of this shell until it receives a SIGCONT signal. The `-f' option means to suspend even if the shell is a login shell.

When job control is not active, the kill and wait built-ins do not accept jobspec arguments. They must be supplied process IDs.

Question 26: man pages

How should I view and search in the man pages?

A: If you want to know how some command is used or if you want more info about a particular command, you don't usually have to search for some text file that contains the help you need. You can read the reference manual for a command by simply typing man, and giving the name of the desired command as an argument to it. Almost every command on a Linux system has a manual page. For example, if you want more info about the ls command, you just type: $ man ls

Many X programs have man pages too. For example, the following gives you the man page for xterm which is a terminal emulator: $ man xterm

Use the following keys and commands for moving around in the manual page:

Command / key	Action
e, j, Enter, or Down	move forward one line
y, k, or Up	move backward one line
f, Space, or Page Down	move forward one page
b, or Page Up	move backward one page
/characters	search the manual page for the specified characters
q	quit

There are manual pages for different programs, utilities, functions and even for some configuration files. The man pages are a very quick and easy way of getting help. The man command itself has a manual page entry, so if you want more info about the man command itself: $ man man

Man pages reference are manual pages and they are usually very brief and technical. The man pages are great if you already know how to use the command and need only a reference or some extra info. They are definitely not tutorials and sometimes they're hard to understand. However, the man pages are very useful because they're always there, only a command away so you should try to learn to use them. The more man pages you read, the more you start to understand them.

Now, what if you need to do a specific task but don't know what program or command to use for the task? Every man page entry contains a short description of the program but the problem is that you don't know what program to use and what man page to read. With the apropos command you can search those descriptions and find the right tool for the job. You can use keywords to search both program names and their descriptions.

Suppose you have a compressed gzip file and you want to uncompress it. You probably want to use a program whose description or name contains the word "gzip". You can use apropos for finding such a program:

```
$ apropos gzip
```
gzip (1) - compress or expand files
zforce (1) - force a '.gz' extension on all gzip files
$

Now when you look at the output of apropos, you probably see that gzip might be what you're looking for. Now you know the command name, and can go read its man page:
```
$ man gzip
```

Although you can do very simple searches with apropos, it's a very powerful tool and you can do advanced searches. For example, you can use the shell wildcards in your searches with the -w option. For more info about apropos, read its man page.

While apropos searches for the descriptions in the man pages, whatis displays the description. It answers the question what is. Of course you can just take a look at the man page of a program to see what the purpose of it is, but if you're only interested in knowing what the program does, you can just use the whatis command for a quick answer:

```
$ whatis apropos
```
apropos (1) - search the manual page names and descriptions
$ whatis man
man (1) - an interface to the on-line reference manuals

man (7) - macros to format man pages
$ whatis whatis
whatis (1) - display manual page descriptions
$

Read the manual page for the man command for more
information about whatis.

Chapter II: Hardware and Architecture

Question 27: The /proc file system

What exactly is /proc file system in LINUX? How does it work?

A: Under Linux, /proc provides information on any running process at /proc/PID. It also includes the ff:

- A symbolic link to the current (traversing) process at /proc/self
- Information on hardware, kernel, and module configuration
- Access to dynamically-configurable kernel options under /proc/sys
- Information about the system as a whole, such as /proc/meminfo, which provides memory statistics.

The basic utilities that use /proc can be located in the procps package. It is required that /proc is mounted in order to function.

The procfs plays an important role in moving functionality from kernel mode to user mode. For example, the GNU version of ps operates entirely in user mode, using the procfs to obtain its data.

The /proc filesystem contains an illusionary filesystem. It does not exist on a disk. Instead, the kernel creates it in memory. It is used to provide information about the system (originally about processes, hence the name). Some of the more important files and directories are explained below. The /proc filesystem is described in more detail in the proc manual page.

/proc/1
     A directory with information about process number 1. Each process has a directory
     below /proc with the name being its process identification number.

/proc/cpuinfo
     Information about the processor, such as its type, make, model, and performance.

/proc/devices
　　List of device drivers configured into the currently running kernel.

/proc/dma
　　Shows which DMA channels are being used at the moment.

/proc/filesystems
　　Filesystems configured into the kernel.

/proc/interrupts
　　Shows which interrupts are in use, and how many of each there has been.

/proc/kcore
　　This represents an image of the physical memory of the system. This is exactly the same size as your physical memory but does not really take up that much memory; it is generated on the fly as programs access it. (Remember: unless you copy it elsewhere, nothing under /proc takes up any disk space at all.)

/proc/kmsg
　　Messages output by the kernel. These are also routed to syslog.

/proc/ksyms
　　Symbol table for the kernel.

/proc/loadavg
　　The `load average' of the system; three meaningless indicators of how much work
　　the system has to do at the moment.

/proc/meminfo
　　Information about memory usage, both physical and swap.

/proc/modules
　　Which kernel modules are loaded at the moment.

/proc/net

Status information about network protocols.

/proc/self
A symbolic link to the process directory of the program that is looking at /proc.
When two processes look at /proc, they get different links. This is mainly a
convenience to make it easier for programs to get at their process directory.

/proc/stat
Various statistics about the system, such as the number of page faults since the
system was booted.

/proc/uptime
The time the system has been up.

/proc/version
The kernel version.

Please take note that while the above files tend to be easily readable text files, they can sometimes be formatted in a way that is not easily digestible. There are many commands that do little more than read the above files and format them for easier understanding.

Question 28: OpenGL - hardware acceleration

I have installed all drivers and I have a problem with Open GL, Quake 3 fps is too low but in Windows 2K it runs fine.

What is the proper procedure to accelerate my hardware?

A: Try to check if 3D hardware acceleration is working for openGL by using the following command:

```
glxinfo |grep rendering
```

This should output "direct rendering: Yes".

If it gives the same but then with "No", hardware 3d acceleration is disabled and all rendering will be done on the CPU.

If it's a 'No', check the following:

Rerun glxinfo with debugging output: In a bash shell this can be done by running:

```
LIBGL_DEBUG=verbose glxinfo
```

This should give some extra info at the top of the output. The common error shown is "permission denied" messages on the drm device. This is often caused by not having loaded the drm kernel module for your video card or there could be some error message in the kernel log when you tried loading it. Another cause can be the permissions set on the drm device. This can be configured in the 'DRI' section of the XF86Config.

Another common error is having multiple libGL library files installed on the system (often caused by installing different drivers and XFree86 versions on top of a current XFree86 install). Check to which libGL glxinfo is linked with:

```
ldd `which glxinfo`
```

This will output a list of libraries then look for a line similar to this one:

```
libGL.so.1 => /usr/X11R6/lib/libGL.so.1 (0x400a2000)
```

Check the file that it's pointing to (this of often a symlink itself, keep following it until you reach the real file). Make sure this libGL library matches your XFree86 version or your card driver. Also check your system of more (non-symlink) libGL files. It often happens that there is one in /usr/lib and another in /usr/X11R6/lib. There should only be one real file and the rest should all be symlinks pointing the correct one.

Question 29: Scan ide devices

I installed a brand new hard drive and issuing the fdisk -l command shows the drive as /dev/hdb.

Is there a way to list the file system?

A: You have to create a partition table and then create a file system in the partition/s.

Enter the cfdisk /dev/hdb command either in your cfdisk (if you have one) or enter the fdisk /dev/hdb command.

Now create a partition and make it type 83. Write the partition table back onto the disk. Exit the cfdisk or fdisk utility.

Next you have to create a file system. This is the same as when you format a partition in Windows. In Linux we use the mkfs command. Do this to create an ext2 file system on /dev/hdb1 if you want to use ext2 file system.

```
root> mkfs -t ext2 -cv /dev/hdb1
```

This command will take some time to end because it also checks the partition for bad blocks as it creates the file system.

Once it's done, then you can mount the file system. Assume you want to mount this file system at /mnt/hdb1. Then you have to create the directory where you want to mount it after which you mount the file system. Note that you only have to create the directory/mount point once.

```
root> mkdir /mnt/hdb1 root> mount /dev/hdb1 /mnt/hdb1
```

Now you can enter the following line in your /etc/fstab file to mount the file system automatically when you restart Linux.

```
/dev/hdb1 /mnt/hdb1 ext2 defaults 0 0
```

If you don't want people from running programs that are on this partition, do this using the noexec option. This would go next to the word defaults in the fstab entry as in:

```
/dev/hdb1 /mnt/hdb1 ext2 defaults,noexec 0 0
```

You can look up all of the mount options by looking at the man page for the mount command and the man page for the fstab file.

Question 30: Partition Table

What does a partition table look like?

A: One may have an arbitrary number of partitions on a disk. However, the Master Boot Record (MBR, sector 0 of the disk) only holds descriptors for 4 partitions, called the primary partitions. Usually the BIOS can boot only from a primary partition. (Of course it can boot a boot loader that itself is able to access non-primary partitions or other disks.) The descriptors for the remaining partitions, called *logical* partitions, are scattered along the disk in a linked list of partition table sectors, starting with the MBR.

Each partition table sector contains 4 partition descriptors. A partition descriptor may be of type 05 (DOS extended partition), 0f (W95 extended partition), 85 (Linux extended partition), or c5 (DRDOS/secured extended partition), in which case it points to another partition table sector. In this way, we obtain a quaternary tree of partitions. Linux accepts 85 as a synonym for 05 - this is useful if one wants to have extended partitions past the 1024 cylinder limit (to prevent DOS fdisk from crashing or hanging). Windows 95 uses 0f for LBA mapped extended partitions. Thus, an extended partition is not a partition containing data, but is a box containing other partitions. Nevertheless, the partition table sector that starts an extended partition has enough room left to contain a boot loader like LILO, so that it is possible to boot an extended partition.

Most operating systems severely restrict the accepted trees. Usually branching is not allowed, and one gets a linear chain of partition table sectors. Linux will accept several extended primary partitions.

Question 31: Advantage of partition

What is the advantage of partitioning my disk?

A: The partition table of a disk cuts it into 'logical disks'. There are several reasons for wanting to do this. DOS does not support filesystems larger than 2 GB, so partitioning is required to break this '2 GB barrier'. Different partitions may carry different operating systems or different filesystems (FAT, HPFS, NTFS, ext2, ...) to be used by one operating system. Sometimes small partitions are used for special purposes (OS/2 Boot Manager uses a small partition for itself; various laptops have a 'hibernation' partition where the state of the system is stored when it goes asleep). Some 'reliable' systems have backup partitions. For backup purposes, say to tape, it is often convenient to have partitions of a size such that the entire partition can be written to a single tape.

It is a good idea to keep your own things (say under /home) and privately installed packages (say under /usr/local) separate from the software installed from a distribution. In case these are on a different partition, it is easier to do a complete reinstall (or switch to a different distribution) without losing your own stuff.

For well-designed systems it is often possible to have all basic system software on a read-only partition, thus diminishing the probability of corruption and saving backup time. There is also a security aspect; for example on a Unix system one might mount all file systems other than the root file system 'nosuid,nodev', and have /tmp, /home, /var not on the root file system, to minimize the possibility that some suid program is tricked into overwriting a vital system file via a hard link to it.

Finally there is the old BIOS problem that can make it impossible to boot a system that lives past cylinder 1024. This may mean that one has to have a partition that ends before the 1024 cylinder limit where the stuff needed at boot time is stored.

Question 32: FDISK/MBR

What do FDISK /MBR do?

A: People often recommend the undocumented DOS command FDISK /MBR to solve problems with the MBR. This command however does not rewrite the entire MBR - it just rewrites the boot code, the first 446 bytes of the MBR, but leaves the 64-byte partition information alone. Thus, it won't help when the partition table has problems. Moreover, it can be dangerous to restore the boot code to its original state: if the cause of the problems was a boot sector virus, then vital information may have been stored elsewhere by the virus and killing the virus may mean killing access to this information. (For example, the stoned.empire.monkey virus encrypts the original MBR to sector 0/0/3.) However, people who want to uninstall LILO, and do not know that LILO has a -u option, can use FDISK /MBR for this purpose.

In a Linux environment, one can wipe all of the MBR with a command like "dd if=/dev/zero of=/dev/hda count=1 bs=512". If only the boot code must be removed, but not the partition table, then "dd if=/dev/zero of=/dev/hda count=1 bs=446" will do. Be very careful with such commands. Usually one regrets them later.

Question 33: Hard drive partitioning

What is hard drive partitioning?

A: Hard disk drive partitioning is the creation of logical divisions upon a hard disk that allows one to apply operating system-specific logical formatting. In simple terms, partitioning a hard drive makes it appear to be more than one hard drive, especially in how each partition is formatted for different operating systems and in how files are copied from one partition to another.

Partitioning allows the creation of several file systems on a single hard disk. This has many benefits, including:

- allowing for dual boot setups (for example, to boot Microsoft Windows and Linux), which means the user can have more than one operating system on his/her computer, although only one can be used at a time; So, you will need at least one partition for Windows and one (actually two) for Linux. In Linux terminology, your entire first hard drive is called /dev/hda and partitions within it are called /dev/hda1, /dev/hda2 and so on. Your original Windows single partition is /dev/hda . The notation for your second hard drive, if you have one, will be /dev/hdb, with partitions within it named /dev/hdb1, /dev/hdb2, etc. Your first SCSI disk, if any, is /dev/sda, etc.

- sharing swap partitions between multiple Linux distributions, which means less hard drive space is wasted on Linux swap partitions, and

- Protection or isolation of files, which means if the operating system stops working, it can just be reinstalled without, hopefully, deleting the user's personal files and settings.

Partitions may be customized to different requirements. One of these is to allow for read-only partitions to protect data. Should one partition be damaged, none of the other file systems are affected and the drive's data may still be salvageable.

There are two types of partition. One of them is primary partition. A primary partition contains one file system. In MS-DOS and earlier versions of Microsoft Windows systems, the first partition (C:) must be a primary partition. Other operating systems may not share this limitation; however, this can depend on other factors such as a PC's BIOS.

Another type is the extended partition, which is able to contain several file systems, known as logical disks (terminology may vary slightly with operating systems).

Question 34: Partition with fdisk

How can I partition my hard drive with the fdisk utility?

A: The following answer shows you how to actually partition your hard drive with the fdisk utility. Linux allows only 4 primary partitions. You can have a much larger number of logical partitions by sub-dividing one of the primary partitions. Only one of the primary partitions can be sub-divided.

The "fdisk" is started by typing (as root) fdisk device at the command prompt. The device might be something like /dev/hda or /dev/sda. The basic fdisk commands you need are:

p- print the partition table

n- create a new partition

d-delete a partition

q-quit without saving changes

w- write the new partition table and exit

Changes you make to the partition table do not take effect until you issue the write (w) command. Here is a sample partition table:

Disk /dev/hdb: 64 heads, 63 sectors, 621 cylinders
Units = cylinders of 4032 * 512 bytes

Device Boot	Start	End	Blocks	Id System
/dev/hdb1 *	1	184	370912+	83 Linux
/dev/hdb2	185	368	370944	83 Linux
/dev/hdb3	369	552	370944	83 Linux
/dev/hdb4	553	621	139104	82 Linux swap

The first line shows the geometry of your hard drive. It may not be physically accurate, but you can accept it as though it were. The hard drive in this example is made of 32 double-sided platters with one head on each side (probably not true). Each platter has 621 concentric tracks. A 3-dimensional track (the same track on all disks) is called a cylinder. Each track is divided into 63 sectors. Each sector contains 512 bytes of data. Therefore the block size in the partition table is 64 heads * 63 sectors * 512 bytes...divided by 1024. The start and end values are cylinders.

Decide on the size of your swap space and where it ought to go. Divide up the remaining space for the three other partitions.

Example:
To start fdisk from the shell prompt:

```
# fdisk /dev/hdb
```

That indicates that you are using the second drive on IDE controller. When you print the (empty) partition table, you'll get configuration information.

Command (m for help): p

Disk /dev/hdb: 64 heads, 63 sectors, 621 cylinders
Units = cylinders of 4032 * 512 bytes

You had a 1.2 GB drive, but now you really know: 64 * 63 * 512 * 621 = 1281982464 bytes. Reserve 128Mb of that space for swap, leaving 1153982464. If you use one of the primary partitions for swap, which means you have three left for ext2 partitions. Divided equally, that makes for 384Mb per partition.

Command (m for help): n
Command action
  e extended
  p primary partition (1-4)

Partition number (1-4): 1
First cylinder (1-621, default 1):<RETURN>
Using default value 1
Last cylinder or +size or +sizeM or +sizeK (1-621, default 621):
+384M

Next, set up the partition you want to use for swap:

Command (m for help): n

Command action
 e extended
 p primary partition (1-4)

Partition number (1-4): 2
First cylinder (197-621, default 197):<RETURN>
Using default value 197
Last cylinder or +size or +sizeM or +sizeK (197-621, default 621):
+128M

Now the partition table will look similar to this:

Device Boot	Start	End	Blocks	Id	System
/dev/hdb1	1	196	395104	83	Linux
/dev/hdb2	197	262	133056	83	Linux

Finally, make the first partition bootable:

Command (m for help): a
Partition number (1-4): 1

And make the second partition of type swap:

Command (m for help): t
Partition number (1-4): 2
Hex code (type L to list codes): 82
Changed system type of partition 2 to 82 (Linux swap)
Command (m for help): p

The end result:
Disk /dev/hdb: 64 heads, 63 sectors, 621 cylinders
Units = cylinders of 4032 * 512 bytes

Device Boot	Start	End	Blocks	Id	System
/dev/hdb1 *	1	196	395104+	83	Linux
/dev/hdb2	197	262	133056	82	Linux swap
/dev/hdb3	263	458	395136	83	Linux
/dev/hdb4	459	621	328608	83	Linux

Finally, issue the write command (w) to write the table on the disk.

Question 35: Dual booting

I recently installed Fedora Core - dual booting with Windows 2000. I plan to buy a new hard drive and install Fedora on it and then just connect the cables to boot into Linux every time I need to use it.

Is this feasible?

A: You can easily achieve dual booting by setting your current drive to master and the new one to slave. To be safe, disconnect the power from the master. Install Linux to the slave drive. Once you're done installing, reboot, test, then re-connect the power to the master drive. Change the setting in the BIOS of your computer rather than switching cables every time you want to change to Linux.

Change the initial boot drive from HDD0 to HDD1 (look at how your BIOS lists them). Windows has to be the first hard drive but Linux will know that it is not "hda"; it will be "hdb" in the case. Also by using this method, you can mount the windows drive into the running Linux install and share files.

Another option is to create a boot disk or cd and only boot from it when you want to load Linux. Or, you can set the bootloader you're using to default to Windows instead of Linux.

Question 36: An easy way to dual boot Windows and Linux

Is there an easy way to dual boot Windows and Linux?

A: The following procedure is applicable if you have a newer pc. This method will not work with older BIOS due to the 1024 cylinder boot limit.

It is assumed that you have an Intel-compatible desktop or notebook with a bootable CD-ROM or DVD drive. You should have at least 128M of RAM. I recommend that you have at least 10G of disk space available for Linux, though 5G would probably be enough.

The latter condition should hold for almost any machine bought in the last five or six years. One other point, though, is that the boot priority should be set so that the machine tries to boot from CD-ROM or DVD before trying to boot from the hard drive. Your machine probably already does this but if not, you can reset the BIOS to do so. Consult your manual on this, or ask at any computer store.

This example will use a 20G HDD and will be installing Windows and Linux Red Hat for concreteness of discussion but the principles should be similar for most other distributions.

Here is our planned partition layout:

1. Windows
2. /boot
3. /swap
4. /

Step I: You will need three things:
1. A Windows 98SE boot disk. This can be created on Windows 98 (control panel > add/remove programs > startup > create boot disk) or alternatively you can search on the internet for one.

2. Microsoft Fdisk. This is again available from Windows

98. Just do a Find Files and folders for 'fdisk' (I think it is in c:\windows\com) and copy the file to floppy.

3. A bootable Windows disk and Linux installation disks

Step II: Partitioning

Before you do the partitioning, I recommend that you run Windows' chkdsk command first in case you have any bad sectors on your hard drive.

Insert your boot disk and boot the PC. Go into your BIOS and set the first boot to Floppy. Save changes and exit.

Your PC should boot and eventually prompt you to make a selection of three options. Choose 2 - Start without the CD ROM support. You can choose 1, but you don't need CD ROM support.

It will take a minute or so and you will end up at the command prompt (A:\). Now insert your disk with 'fdisk' on it and type: fdisk. You will then be prompted whether you want large disk support. Select 'Yes'

Now you will be presented with some options.

Select option 1: Create a DOS partition of logical dos drive.

The next screen will give you three options.

Select option 1 again: Create Primary DOS partition. Now you're going to create a Primary partition. If asked to use *all* space, answer 'No' and enter the amount you wish for the C: drive. If you want 12Gigs, enter: 12000

The first partition on your first hard drive should automatically be set to Active partition. If not, FDISK may ask you, or you may have to select item 2: Set active partition from the main menu.

You can also go back and delete it if you made the wrong choice.

There are two things you can do from here. You can create the other partitions or continue and create the other partitions when installing Linux. If you want to create the partitions now, read the next step otherwise skip to Step V.

Step III: Create extended and logical partitions:

After creating the first partition, we now go back to the main menu and select option 1 again: Create a DOS partition of logical dos drive.

Now we select option 2: Create Extended DOS partition. This partition will hold the swap, /boot and root.

When prompted to enter the amount, use *all* the space left. If you don't, you'll wind up with unused space on your hard drive.

After doing so, FDISK should automatically advance to the next step -> creating Logical DOS drives. It should give you a message that says something like "This drive has no Logical DOS drives. Would you like to create some now?"

The logical DOS drives are just all the partitions within the extended partition.

Select 'Yes'. Now enter the first amount. If you want 70MB for your boot, then type 70. Now create another one and enter 512 for your swap. Again, enter the remaining space which will be your root (/).

Step IV: Formatting the drive for Windows:

Now, exit from the fids menu, put your boot-disk back in and reboot. Select option 2 and when arriving at the prompt (A:\) type: format c:

This will format the drive for installation. When finished, reboot the computer (make sure you take out the floppy). Go into the BIOS and set the first boot to your CD ROM.

Now put your Windows CD in and save the changes you have made to the BIOS. Windows will boot and install from the CD. After installation, don't worry about installing all your drivers, you can do that later.

Step V: Installing Linux:

Now reboot the computer with your Linux disk 1 in the CD ROM. Make sure that your first boot device is set to CD.

Run the installation program. When prompted to partition, you can just use the existing partitions and assign them to swap, boot and /. Otherwise you can create the partitions from within the program by manual partitioning. Make the partitions to suit you preferred sizes and assign them to their mount points. Continue with the installation.

When prompted to install a bootloaded, choose GRUB if it is there. LILO will also work fine but GRUB is better. Make sure you install the bootloader on the Master Boot Record (MBR), otherwise you will not have a boot option screen to boot Linux and Windows.

When prompted to make a boot disk, insert a floppy and let it create a boot disk.

When finished, reboot and you are done.

Question 37: Confirm PSU status

I had a Redhat installed in my pc. During BIOS boot a battery missing can be seen.

How can I confirm the battery or psu status in the OS environment?

A: The information you are after are in the /proc directory and under /proc/acpi. You can do cat /proc/cpuinfo to see what is in the file.

I also suggest writing down all the information that you see in the BIOS and get a new battery. To check the voltage of the CMOS battery, use lm_sensors. The voltage will not tell you that it is dead. You need a button battery checker to test if it is still good or bad.

Question 38: Disable driver verifier

I'm having an error that is related to drivers but I am unable to find any conflicts. I have tried disabling all new hardware, but to no avail.

How can I disable the driver verifier?

A: To set file signature verification options, you can do the ff:

1. Open System in Control Panel.
2. On the Hardware tab, click Driver Signing.
3. Under File signature verification, click one of the following:

- Ignore to allow all device drivers to be installed on this computer, regardless of whether they have a digital signature.

- Warn to display a warning message whenever an installation program attempts to install a device driver without a digital signature. This is the default behavior for Windows.

- Block to prevent an installation program from installing device drivers without a digital signature.

If you are a logged on as an administrator or as a member of the Administrators group, under Administrator option, click Apply setting as system default to apply the selected setting as the default for all users who log on to this computer.

Question 39: SCSI

What is a SCSI?

A: SCSI stands for Small Computer System Interface. It's a standard for connecting peripherals to your computer via a standard hardware interface which uses standard SCSI commands. The SCSI standard can be divided into SCSI (SCSI1) and SCSI2 (SCSI wide and SCSI wide and fast) and now SCSI-3 which is made up of at least 14 separate standards documents.

SCSI2 is the most popular version of the SCSI command specification and allows for scanners, hard disk drives, CD-ROM players, tapes and many other devices. SCSI-3 resolves many "gray areas" and adds much new functionality and performance improvements. It also adds new types of SCSI busses like fiber channel which uses a 4 pin copper connection or a pair of glass fiber optic cables instead of the familiar ribbon cable connection.

Question 40: Choosing SCSI Devices

I want to use a SCSI interface but how do I choose what devices should I utilize?

A: I suggest for you to have devices which use LVD, automatic termination and SCAM (SCSI Configured Automatically). Most new devices fit this pattern. Also make sure that you consider where these devices are going to go, since you need to consider the total length of the cable. And check to see if you will need an adapter for an external device (50 to 25 pin or 68 to 50 pin).

Buy quality SCSI cards and PCI if possible. Make sure it will support the bus speed you have in mind (SCSI-3 U2W for example). I recommend Adaptec cards as the best on the market but I have also heard good things about the Diamond cards. Also make sure you buy high quality cables. Granite Digital makes great cables and other accessories and is well known for their quality.

A SCSI hard drive is set-up just like any other drive. Depending on your BIOS settings, you can set the system to boot from the SCSI drive or from an IDE drive. There is no problem in using a mixed drive setup. Seagate, IBM and Quantum are all well known for their SCSI drives.

A great number of manufacturers offer SCSI burners (CD-R or CD-RW) but just plain CD players are harder to come by.

A good high-end scanner will be a SCSI scanner. Check around to see what kind of results people are getting with the model you have in mind.

Zip Drives, LS120s, Jaz Drives and many other devices of this type are available in the SCSI interface. You can add any SCSI device into your chain as long as you have not exceeded the number of devices for your card.

Question 41: Setting up a SCSI chain

How do I set up a SCSI chain?

A: Install the SCSI card. Most cards today are plug_and_play and Windows will find and configure them quickly and easily. The next step is to cable the devices together and set the I.D.s and termination (if necessary). Each device on a SCSI chain requires its own I.D.

As an example (example is an 8 device chain):

ID#0 - hard drive
ID#1 - CD-ROM
ID#2 - CD-R
ID#3 - Internal Jaz
ID#4 - Scanner
ID#5 - Hard drive
ID#6 - Zip
ID#7 - SCSI Card

If two devices are set to have the same I.D., the whole chain may not work or possibly just the conflicting devices. Always make sure each device has a different I.D. Most devices have jumpers or a small dial for setting the I.D. number. The hard drive at ID#0 should be your boot drive (if you are booting SCSI), and the CD-ROM is set at the lowest available I.D.# in order to have it assigned a drive letter before the CD-R.

Termination is a separate issue, but it also affects your SCSI bus a great deal. Each device at the far ends of a SCSI chain must be terminated. This refers to their physical location on the chain and NOT their ID number. In the above example, the scanner is probably at one end of the chain and possibly a hard drive is at the other with the card in the middle, like so:

Scanner
ZIP
Card
CD-ROM
CD-R

Jaz
Hard drive
Hard drive

So, unless the devices are auto-terminating, that hard drive and the scanner must be set to terminate usually by jumpers or a switch on the device. In older devices, this might actually require placing a terminator on the end of the chain. Generally, that is no longer necessary. All items between the ends must have their termination disabled or the chain will not operate properly. If you have all internal devices or all external devices, then the card itself will be an end device and must be terminated. If you have a couple of auto termination devices, and a few which are not, you can try to set the auto termination devices at the ends of the chain to make setup easier.

Despite the reputation of being difficult to configure, I have found that SCSI is extremely easy to get up and running. Pay attention to the issues above and you should be fine. Just in case, here are a few troubleshooting tips:

- Check Termination First. Then check it again.

- Check ID numbers

- Use quality cables. If you have a problem especially with a fast hard drive, try changing the cable.

- Use the shortest connections possible. Pay attention to the maximum total length.

- Make sure you have the newest ASPI drivers (Adaptec site if you have an Adaptec card).

- Make sure the cables are plugged in correctly and firmly: pin 1 to pin 1.

- If you are not sure your devices are SCAM compliant, turn it off.

- Check for IRQ conflicts.

Question 42: Changing screen resolution

I installed mdv 2006 and it works fine at 1024X768. I wanted to raise the resolution but when I do, the window is larger than my screen. I have to drag the mouse pointer to see the top or bottom of the screen or left and right.

What is the best way to change the screen resolution?

A: There are a couple of things you can do:

1. Install all the updates available. There are several updates to the graphical system called "X" or "xorg". Mdv2006 shipped with a developmental version of xorg that caused problems with some nvidia based cards. Later updates fixed that.

2. The configuration file for your graphical system is /etc/X11/xorg.conf. This is a fairly lengthy file divided into sections.

3. After you installing all the updates, rerun the graphical configuration utility. You can do so by opening a console and run:

```
$ su
<enter root password>
# XFdrake
```

A window will pop up with XFdrake, the mandriva graphics setup utility. Check that you have the right card selected and double check your monitor setting. There is a button you can press to test the configuration changes you make before committing them. Keep trying until you get something that tests out properly. Actually, you might want to try running XFdrake before doing anything else. By the way, XFdrake automatically edits xorg.conf for you thus simplifying the graphics setup process.

4. Mandriva ships with the open source driver for your nvidia

based graphics card called "nv". That's probably what you will
see in your xorg.conf "Device" section for the driver. Nvidia
makes an excellent closed source Linux driver but the
installation is a little daunting for newbie's. You need the nvidia
driver for 3d acceleration necessary to run many games. After
you get things running properly with the open source driver, you
may want to consider installing the nvidia closed source driver.

Question 43: Modem

What is a Modem?

A: A modem is a device that lets one send digital signals over an ordinary telephone line not designed for digital signals. If all telephone lines are digital, then you wouldn't need a modem. But sometimes, a substitute for an analog modem, connected to a digital phone line is inaccurately called a "digital modem". A modem permits your computer to connect to and communicate with the rest of the world. When you use a modem, you normally use a communication program or web browser to utilize the modem and dial-out on a telephone line. Advanced modem users can set things up so that others may phone in to them and use the computer remotely. This is called "dial-in".

Oversimplified, there are four basic types of analog modems for a PC: external serial (RS-232), USB (= external USB), internal, and built-in. The external serial and USB set on your desk outside the PC while the other two types are not visible since they're inside the PC. The external serial modem plugs into a connector on the back of the PC known as a "serial port". The USB modem plugs into a USB cable. The internal modem is a card that is inserted inside the computer. The built-in modem is a chip on the motherboard used primarily in laptops. Internal modems will generally apply also to built-in modems. Internal modems are further subdivided into PCI, ISA, and AMR depending on whether they are designed for the PCI or ISA bus or for an AMR slot.

When you get an internal or built-in modem, you also get a dedicated serial port (which can only be used with the modem and not with anything else such as an external modem or console terminal). In Linux, the common serial ports are named ttyS0, ttyS1, etc. (or tts/0, tts/1 for the device file system (devfs).

Modems usually include the ability to send Faxes (Fax Modems) while "Voice" modems can work like an automatic answering machine and handle voicemail.

Question 44: Identify software modem

How do you determine if an internal modem is a software modem?

A: First see if the name, description or even the name of the MS Windows driver for it indicates it's a software modem: HSP (Host Signal Processor) , HCF (Host Controlled Family), HSF (Host Signal Family), controller less, host-controlled, host-based, and soft modem. If it's one of these modems, it will only work for the cases where a Linux driver is available. Since software modems cost less, a low price is a clue that it's a software modem.

If you don't know the model of the modem and you also have Windows on your Linux PC, click on the "Modem" icon in the "Control Panel". Then see the modem list. If the above doesn't work, you can look at the package the modem came in. Read the section on the package that says something like "Minimum System Requirements" or just "System Requirements".

A hardware modem will work fine on old CPUs (such as the 386 or better). So if it requires a modern CPU (such as a Pentium or other "high speed" CPU of say over 150 MHz) this is a clue that it's an all-software modem. If it only requires a 486 CPU (or better) then it's likely a host-controlled software modem.

You may have a hardware modem if it fails to state explicitly that you must have Windows. By saying its "designed for Windows" it may only mean that it fully supports Microsoft's plug-and-play which is okay since Linux uses the same plug-and-play specs. Being "designed for Windows" thus gives no clue as to whether or not it will work under Linux. You might check the Website of the manufacturer or inquire via email. Some manufacturers are specifically stating that certain models work under Linux. Sometimes they are linmodems that require you to obtain and install a certain linmodem driver.

Question 45: sound application error

The sound applications do not work properly when I run Linux then boot DOS.

Why does this happen?

A. That happens after a soft reboot to DOS. Sometimes the error message misleadingly refers to a bad CONFIG.SYS file. Most of the current sound cards have software programmable IRQ and DMA settings. If you use different settings between Linux and MS-DOS/Windows, this may cause problems. Some sound cards don't accept new parameters without a complete reset.

A fast solution to this problem is to perform a full reboot using the reset button or power cycle rather than a soft reboot (e.g. Ctrl-Alt-Del).

The correct solution is to ensure that you use the same IRQ and DMA settings with MS-DOS and Linux (or not to use DOS).

Question 46: Configure Linux to support sound

What are the correct steps to configure Linux to support sound?

A: Follow these steps:

1. Installing the sound card: Follow the manufacturer's instructions for installing the hardware or have your dealer perform the installation. Older sound cards usually have switch or jumper settings for IRQ, DMA channel, etc; note down the values used. Use the factory defaults if you are not sure. Try to avoid conflicts with other devices (e.g. Ethernet cards, SCSI host adaptors, serial and parallel ports) if possible. Usually you should use the same I/O port, IRQ, and DMA settings that work under DOS. In some cases, you may need to use different settings to get things to work under Linux. A trial and error may be needed.

2. Configuring Plug and Play if applicable: Some sound cards use the ISA Plug and Play protocol to configure settings for I/O addresses, interrupts, and DMA channels. If you have a newer PCI-bus type of sound card or one of the very old ISA sound cards that uses fixed settings or jumpers, then you can skip this procedure. The preferred way to configure Plug and Play cards is to use the isapnp tools which ship with most Linux distributions or download them from Red Hat's web site http://www.redhat.com/.

First check the documentation for your Linux distribution. It may already have Plug and Play support set up for you or it may work slightly differently than described here. If you need to configure it yourself, the details can be found in the man pages for the isapnp tools. Briefly the process you would normally follow is:

- Use pnpdump to capture the possible settings for all your Plug and Play devices, saving the result to the file /etc/isapnp.conf.
- Choose settings for the sound card that do not conflict with any other devices in your system and uncomment

the appropriate lines in /etc/isapnp.conf. Don't forget to uncomment the (ACT Y) command near the end.

- Make sure that isapnp is run when your system boots up, normally done by one of the startup scripts. Reboot your system or run isapnp manually.

If for some reason you cannot or do not wish to use the isapnp tools, there are a couple of other options. If you use the card under Microsoft Windows 95 or 98, you can use the device manager to set up the card, then soft boot into Linux using the LOADLIN program. Make sure Windows and Linux use the same card setup parameters. If you use the card under DOS, you can use the icu utility that comes with SoundBlaster16 PnP cards to configure it under DOS, then soft boot into Linux using the LOADLIN program. Again, make sure DOS and Linux use the same card setup parameters. True ISA PnP support is implemented in the 2.4 and later kernels. Some of the sound card drivers now support automatically detecting and configuring the cards without the isapnp tools. Check the documentation for the card's driver for details.

3. Configuring and building the kernel for sound support: You need the appropriate device drivers for your sound card to be present in the kernel. The kernel running on your system may already include the drivers for your sound card. In most cases the drivers would have been built as kernel loadable modules. You can check which drivers are available as modules by looking in the /lib/modules directories. For the 2.4.4 kernel, the sound drivers would normally appear in /lib/modules/2.4.4/kernel/drivers/sound/. If you see the driver(s) for your sound card, you can try using the module directory and skip recompiling the kernel.

If the sound drivers are not already built, you will need to configure and build a new kernel. You can either build the sound drivers into the kernel or build them as kernel loadable modules. In most cases building as modules is preferred, as it allows you to easily experiment with loading different drivers if unsure which one to use and the drivers can be unloaded when not needed, freeing up memory. Building the drivers into the kernel itself may be desirable if you are unfamiliar with kernel modules and want a simpler solution.

If you have never configured the kernel for sound support before it is a good idea to read the relevant documentation included with the kernel sound drivers, particularly information specific to your card type. The files can be found in the kernel documentation directory and usually installed in /usr/src/linux/Documentation/sound. If this directory is missing, you likely either have a very old kernel version or you have not installed the kernel source code. Follow the usual procedure for building the kernel. There are currently three interfaces to the configuration process. A graphical user interface that runs under X11 can be invoked using make xconfig. A menu-based system that only requires text displays is available as make menuconfig. The original method, using make config, offers a simple text-based interface.

When configuring the kernel there will be many choices for selecting the type of sound card you have and the driver options to use. The on-line help within the configuration tool should provide an explanation of what each option is for. Select the appropriate options to the best of your knowledge. After configuring the options you should compile and install the new kernel as per the Kernel HOWTO.

4. Creating the device files: For proper operation, device file entries must be created for the sound devices. These are normally created for you during installation of your Linux system. A quick check can be made using the command listed below. If the output is as shown (the date stamp will vary) then the device files are almost certainly okay.

```
% ls -l /dev/dsp
crw-rw-rw-   1 root      root      14,   3 Jan 25  1997
/dev/dsp
```

Note that having the right device files there doesn't guarantee anything on its own. The kernel driver must also be loaded or compiled in before the devices will work.

In rare cases, if you believe the device files are wrong, you can recreate them. Most Linux distributions have a /dev/MAKEDEV script which can be used for this purpose.

Take note that if you are using the devfs filesystem support in the 2.4 kernels, the sound device files are actually found in /dev/sound, but there will be symbolic links to the older devices, such as /dev/dsp.

5. Booting the Linux kernel and testing the installation: You should now be ready to boot the new kernel and test the sound drivers. Follow your usual procedure for installing and rebooting the new kernel.

If you are using loadable kernel modules for sound, you will need to load them using the modprobe command for the appropriate drivers, e.g. run the command modprobe sb for a SoundBlaster card.

After booting or loading the kernel modules, check for a message such as the following using the dmesg command:

```
Soundblaster audio driver Copyright (C) by Hannu
Savolainen 1993-1996
sb: Creative SB AWE64  PnP detected
sb: ISAPnP reports 'Creative SB AWE64  PnP' at i/o 0x220,
irq 5, dma 1, 5
SB 4.16 detected OK (220)
sb: 1 Soundblaster PnP card(s) found.

Crystal 4280/46xx + AC97 Audio, version 1.22.32, 10:28:40
Apr 28 2001
cs46xx: Card found at 0xf4100000 and 0xf4000000, IRQ 11
cs46xx: Thinkpad 600X/A20/T20 (1014:0153) at
0xf4100000/0xf4000000, IRQ 11
ac97_codec: AC97 Audio codec, id: 0x4352:0x5914 (Cirrus
Logic CS4297A rev B)
```

The message should indicate that a sound card was found and match your sound card type and jumper settings (if any). The driver may also display some error messages and warnings if you have incorrectly configured the driver or chosen the wrong one.

Previous versions of this HOWTO suggested checking the output of /dev/sndstat. This is no longer supported in the 2.4 and later kernels.

Now you should be ready to play a simple sound file. Get hold of a sound sample file, and send it to the sound device as a basic check of sound output, e.g.

```
% cat endoftheworld >/dev/dsp
% cat crash.au >/dev/audio
```

(Make sure you don't omit the ">" in the commands above).

Note that using cat is not the proper way to play audio files; it's just a quick check. You'll want to get a proper sound player program that will do a better job.

If the above commands return "I/O error", you should look at the end of the kernel messages listed using the "dmesg" command. It's likely that an error message is printed there. Very often the message is "Sound: DMA (output) timed out - IRQ/DRQ config error?" The message means that the driver didn't get the expected interrupt from the sound card. In most cases it means that the IRQ or the DMA channel configured to the driver doesn't work. The best way to get it working is to try with all possible DMAs and IRQs supported by the device.

Another possible reason is that the device is not compatible with the device the driver is configured for. This is almost certainly the case when a supposedly "SoundBlaster (Pro/16) compatible" sound card doesn't work with the SoundBlaster driver. In this case you should try to find out the device your sound card is compatible with.

If you have sound input capability, you can do a quick test of this using command such as the following:

```
# record 4 seconds of audio from microphone
% dd bs=8k count=4 </dev/audio >sample.au
4+0 records in
4+0 records out
# play back sound
% cat sample.au >/dev/audio
```

Obviously for this to work you need a microphone connected to the sound card and you should speak into it. You may also need to obtain a mixer program to set the microphone as the input device and adjust the recording gain level.

If these tests pass, you can be reasonably confident that the sound D/A or A/D hardware and software are working.

Some Linux distributions provide a sound driver configuration utility that will detect your sound card and set up the entire necessary configuration files to load the appropriate sound drivers for your card. Red Hat Linux, for example, provides the sndconfig utility. If your distribution provides such a tool I suggest you try using it.

Chapter III: Installing Software

Question 47: Red Hat Package manager

What is RPM?

A: RPM stands for Red Hat Package Manager. However, these days RPM isn't only Red Hat specific because many other Linux distros use RPM for managing their software. For example, both Mandriva and SuSE use RPM for software management. With RPM, you can install, upgrade and uninstall software on Linux, as well as keep track of already installed RPM packages on your system. This can be done because RPM keeps a database of all software that was installed with it.

RPM uses software packages that have the .rpm extension. An RPM package contains the actual software that gets installed, maybe some additional files for the software, information on where the software and its files get installed and a list of other files you need to have on your system in order to run this specific piece of software.

When you use RPM for installing the software package, RPM checks if your system is suitable for the software the RPM package contains, figures out where to install the files the package provides, installs them on your system and adds that piece of software into its database of installed RPM packages.

Different Linux distros may keep their software and the files related to that software in different directories. That's why it's important to use the RPM package that was made for your distribution. For example, if you install a SuSE specific software package on a Red Hat system, RPM may put the files from that package into wrong directories. In the worst case the result is that the program doesn't find all the files it needs and doesn't work properly.

Note that you need to be root when installing software in Linux. When you've got the root privileges, you use the rpm command with appropriate options to manage your RPM software packages.

Question 48: Installing and upgrading RPM packages

What is the proper procedure tin install and upgrade RPM packages?

A: Use the rpm command with -i option (which stands for "install") for installing a software package. For example, to install an RPM package called software-2.3.4.rpm:
rpm -i software-2.3.4.rpm

If you already have some version installed on your system and want to upgrade it to the new version, use -U option (which stands for "upgrade"). For example, if you have software-2.3.3.rpm installed and wants to upgrade it:
rpm -U software-2.3.4.rpm

If nothing goes wrong, the files in your package will get installed into your system and you can run your new program. Note that rpm doesn't usually create a special directory for the software package's files. Instead, the different files from the package get placed into appropriate existing directories on your Linux system. Executable programs go usually into /bin, /usr/bin, /usr/X11/bin, or /usr/X11R6/bin after installing with rpm.

Sometimes the program gets automatically added into your menu but usually you can just run the program by typing its name at the command prompt. In most cases you don't have to know where the program was installed because you don't have to type the whole path when running the program, only the program's name is needed.

Question 49: Error: failed dependencies

The RPM stopped installing and I'm getting a dependency error.

How do I resume installation?

A: Many Linux programs need other files or programs in order to work properly. A piece of software depends on other software. When you try to install an RPM package, RPM automatically checks its database for other files that the software being installed needs. If RPM can't find those files in its database, it stops installing the software and complains about failed dependencies.

RPM gives out a list of files the program needs when you get a dependency error. The files in the list are probably ones you don't have on your system or files that you have but are the wrong versions. You will have to find the files RPM complains about, install or upgrade those files first and then try to install the package you were installing.

If the needed files are there and still get a failed dependency error, use the --nodeps option. This tells RPM not to check any dependencies before installing the package:

```
# rpm -i software-2.3.4.rpm --nodeps
```

This forces RPM to ignore dependency errors and install software anyway but if the needed files are not there, the program won't work well or won't work at all. Use the --nodeps option only when you know that the needed files are there.

Question 50: Removing software installed with RPM

What is the correct method to remove software installed with RPM?

A: To remove software that was installed with RPM, use the -e option (erase): `# rpm -e software-2.3.4.`

You don't have to type the whole name of the package that contained the software and you don't have to type the .rpm extension when removing software. Probably, you don't have to type the version number either, so this would do exactly the same as the -e option: # rpm -e software

This rpm -e command uses the RPM database to check where all the files related to this software were installed and then automatically removes all of those files. After removing the program files, it also removes the program from the database of installed software.

It is very important that you never remove RPM software manually (for example, deleting single files with rm). If you just run around your system randomly deleting files that were installed with RPM, you'll get rid of the software but RPM doesn't know it and doesn't remove the software package from its database. The result is that RPM still thinks the program is installed on your system and you may run into dependency problems later.

If you used RPM for installing a certain piece of software, also use RPM for removing that piece of software.

Question 51: Querying the RPM database

How can I the list of packages in the RPM database?

A: You can query the RPM database to get info of the packages on your Linux system. To query a single package, use the -q option. For example, to query a package whose name is "software": # `rpm -q software`

After issuing this command, rpm either tells you the version of the package or that the package isn't installed.

If you want a list of all packages installed on your system, you'll have to query all with -qa: # `rpm -qa`

If you are given a long list, you'll need a way to scroll it. The best way is to pipe the list to less: # `rpm -qa | less`

If you're looking for packages whose names contain a specific word, you can use grep for finding those packages. For example, to get a list of all installed RPM packages whose names contain the word "kde", do something like this: # `rpm -qa | grep kde`

The above command makes rpm list all packages in its database and pass the list to grep. Then grep checks every line for "kde" and finally shows you all the lines that contain the word "kde".

Question 52: Installing software from source in Linux

Is it easy to compile and install software from source in Linux?

A: Yes, it is. Compiling and installing software from source in Linux isn't as hard as it may sound.

The installation procedure for software that comes in tar.gz and tar.bz2 packages isn't always the same but usually it's like this:

```
# tar xvzf package.tar.gz (or tar xvjf
package.tar.bz2)
# cd package
# ./configure
# make
# make install
```

By issuing these simple commands you can unpack, configure, compile, and install the software package and you don't even have to know what you're doing. However, it's best to have a clear understanding of the installation procedure and see what these steps stand for.

Step 1. Unpacking:
The package containing the source code of the program has a tar.gz or a tar.bz2 extension. This means that the package is a compressed tar archive also known as a tarball. When making the package, the source code and the other needed files were piled together in a single tar archive, hence the tar extension. After piling them all together in the tar archive, the archive was compressed with gzip, thus the gz extension.

Some people want to compress the tar archive with bzip2 instead of gzip. In these cases, the package has a tar.bz2 extension. You can install these packages exactly the same way as tar.gz packages but use a bit different command when unpacking.

It doesn't matter where you put the tarballs you download from the internet but I suggest creating a special directory for downloaded tarballs. You can put your downloaded tar.gz or tar.bz2 software packages into any directory you want. In this example I assume your username is Larry and you've downloaded a package called pkg.tar.gz into the dls directory you've created (/home/larry/dls).

After downloading the package, you unpack it with this command:

```
me@puter: ~/dls$ tar xvzf pkg.tar.gz
```

As you can see, you use the tar command with the appropriate options (xvzf) for unpacking the tarball. If you have a package with tar.bz2 extension instead, you must tell tar that this isn't a gzipped tar archive. You do so by using the j option instead of z like this:

```
me@puter: ~/dls$ tar xvjf pkg.tar.bz2
```

What happens after unpacking depends on the package. In most cases, a directory with the package's name is created. The newly created directory goes under the directory where you are right now. To be sure, you can give the ls command:

```
larry@puter: ~/dls$ ls
pkg pkg.tar.gz
larry@puter: ~/dls$
```

In our example unpacking our package pkg.tar.gz did what is expected and created a directory with the package's name. Now you must cd into that newly created directory:

```
larry@puter: ~/dls$ cd pkg
larry@puter: ~/dls/pkg$
```

It is very important to read any documentation you find in this directory like README or INSTALL files before continuing.

Step 2. Configuring:
After you've changed into the package's directory, it's time to configure the package. Usually but not always, it's done by running this configure script:

```
larry@puter: ~/dls/pkg$ ./configure
```

Issuing the configure script doesn't compile anything yet but checks your system and assigns values for system-dependent variables. These values are used for generating a Makefile. The Makefile in turn is used for generating the actual binary.

If configure finds an error, it complains about it and exits. However, if everything works like it should, configure doesn't complain about anything. If configure exited without errors, then it's time to move on to the next step.

Step 3. Building:
It's finally time to actually build the binary, the executable program, from the source code. This is done by running the make command: larry@puter: ~/dls/pkg$ make

Note that make needs the Makefile for building the program. Otherwise it doesn't know what to do. This is why it's so important to run the configure script successfully or generate the Makefile in some other way.

When you run make, you'll see again a bunch of strange messages filling your screen. This is also perfectly normal and nothing you should worry about. This step may take some time, depending on how big the program is and how fast your computer is.

If all goes as it should, your executable is finished and ready to run after make has done its job. Now, the final step is to install the program.

Step 4: Installing
Now it's time to install the program. When doing this you must be root. If you've done things as a normal user, you can become root with the su command. It'll ask you the root password and then you're ready for the final step.

```
larry@puter: ~/dls/pkg$ su
Password:
root@puter: /home/larry/dls/pkg#
```

Now when you're root, you can install the program with the make install command:

```
root@puter: /home/larry/dls/pkg# make install
```

Again, you'll get some weird messages scrolling on the screen. After it has stopped, you have successfully installed the software.

In this example, we didn't change the behavior of the configure script, the program was installed in the default place. In many cases it's /usr/local/bin. If /usr/local/bin (or whatever place your program was installed in) is already in your PATH, you can just run the program by typing its name.

If you became root with su, you'd better get back your normal user privileges before you do something else. Type exit to become a normal user again:

```
root@puter: /home/me/dls/pkg# exit
exit
larry@puter: ~/dls/pkg$
```

Question 53: Cleaning up the mess

How do I get rid of unwanted files after installing software from source in Linux?

A: When you ran "make", it created all sorts of files that were needed during the build process but are useless now and are just taking up disk space. This is why you'll want to make clean:

```
me@puter: ~/dls/pkg$ make clean
```

However, make sure you keep your Makefile. It's needed if you later decide to uninstall the program and want to do it as less troublesome as possible.

Question 54: Uninstalling

I want to uninstall the programs I compiled by myself, what is the method for doing this?

A: Uninstalling the programs you've compiled yourself is not as easy as uninstalling programs you've installed with a package manager, like rpm.

The first step is to read the documentation that came with your software package and see if it says anything about uninstalling. If you didn't delete your Makefile, you may be able to remove the program by doing a make uninstall:

```
root@puter: /home/me/dls/pkg# make uninstall
```

If you see weird text scrolling on your screen that's a good sign. If "make" starts complaining, that's a bad sign. Then you'll have to remove the program files manually.

If you know where the program was installed, you'll have to manually delete the installed files or the directory where your program is. If you have no idea where all the files are, you'll have to read the Makefile and see where all the files got installed and then delete them.

Chapter IV: Linux Installation, Package Management

Question 55: Pre-Installation

What should I know before I install Linux?

A: If you have a Live-CD version of your system (most of the modern distros have it), download it and run it before installing the system on your hard drive. This may help you identify possible problems with your hardware (some of it may be unsupported under Linux) and just have an impression about the general usability of the selected distro without the need of installing it on your disk and without losing any data.

You have to know that Linux requires a free partition on your disk to be installed properly. If you have Windows installed and have only one system partition (just the C: drive), then you can either resize your partition or completely remove Windows. Some installers support Windows partitions resizing, but not all. If you wish to install a distro which doesn't support it, you have to do it manually before the installation. There are many tools for changing the partition size. One of the most popular is a commercial app called Partition Magic. You don't have to use it though, because most Linux Live-CDs include a partitioning program (qtparted or GParted) capable of resizing Windows partitions.

Be warned that in many installers, the default value for partitioning is to completely format your hard drive removing all your data (if any) and create the Linux partitions on the clean space. This is not the desired behavior if you have another system or some important data on your disk. In this case you should not agree to clean the disk, but choose either the option "Use the free space" or "format manually". It is absolutely necessary to read the installer tips carefully to avoid problems later on.

Some distros (the minority) do not have any partitioning program (they can only install on already existing partitions). In this case you also have to partition your hard drive manually beforehand.

Once upon a time, the installer may crash or refuse to continue working properly. This may be due to a badly burned CD-ROM or due to some installer bug. It may be also that some uncommon piece of hardware is causing the installer to behave in an unstable way. There may be many reasons for crashing. It happens pretty rarely nowadays on the desktop machines, more often on laptops. In case you're installing on a mobile computer, you can read the laptop tips which may help you to diagnose the problem and install Linux on your machine.

Question 56: Sharing Disk

Is it possible for GNU/Linux and MS Windows to share disk?

A: When we talk about GNU/Linux and Microsoft Windows in terms of co-existence on the same physical machine or to be more precise - on the same hard drive, one should be aware that it is not very difficult to achieve that goal. In most cases it is being done automatically by the Linux installation process itself.

Software responsible for choosing correct operation system during computer boot sequence is called boot manager. In most cases that small program is positioned in master boot record (MBR) of the hard drive or alternatively in the very first sector of one of existing partitions on the disk. Microsoft has embedded his own boot manager into Windows but unfortunately it is not capable of running any other systems then those from Microsoft Windows family. That is why, in most cases, our choice of boot manager will be limited to Linux system (e.g. LILO or Grub).

Question 57: Bootloader

What does a bootloader do?

A: The program which loads the kernel into the memory at the boot time is called bootloader. The bootloaders that come with Linux distributions are LILO and GRUB. If you want change LILO configuration, you have to open the file /etc/lilo.conf. using your favorite editor. In this file each line has its meaning.

boot=/dev/hda	Install LILO in the MBR
prompt	If you want select another section
timeout=50	Wait five seconds before booting
default=linux	The section to boot after the timeout

image=/boot/vmlinuz-x.x.x	
label=Linux	Name we give to this section
read-only	Start with a read-only root
root=/dev/hda3	Location of the root filesystem

other=/dev/hdaX	The host where Windows is installed
label=windows	

Question 58: safe place for boot manager

Where is the best place to install a boot manager?

A: The best and the safest place to install boot manager is a first sector of master boot record (MBR) and in most cases that is a default option. That gives us a list of mostly all available systems to be booted during computer boot sequence. There are more options worth our consideration:

1. Have the boot manager installed on a floppy disk or a Flash memory. This is very useful in case of loosing the MBR from the hard drive or any other reason.

2. Have the boot manager installed on the first sector of any portion of your drive, in this case we will have to point our main boot manager to any other boot manager programs located on our drive. That way we can gain ability to run from one boot manager other boot managers. This would be useful in case of having boot managers for particular systems, e.g., having compiled different kernels for the same system and still having different operation systems on our computer. This case allows us to write a boot menu in our MBR with up to four systems.

Question 59: Recover boot manager

What will happen when Windows had already removed boot manager?

A: When we want to have two systems on our hard drive, it is more comfortable to install MS Windows first. There is a known problem with Microsoft's operation systems which do not see anything except itself. Linux systems are friendlier and are more able to co-exist with systems already installed on a hard drive. During installation user is being asked a question whether new Linux system should be installed on the whole available space or should occupy only unused part of the hard drive. If that is the option chosen by us, Linux will create new partition for itself and get installed without interfering with other systems.

When we installed MS Windows after Linux installation, it is more than probable that Windows had already overwritten default boot manager. In that case, we have to recover boot manager in a way allowing us to normally boot both systems.

There are few possibilities available to be able to cope with that problem. One of the easiest ways is to insert a LiveCD of our distribution into CD or DVD drive and then mount root partition of our Linux system using chroot tool, changing for root directory of our distribution. If we assume that our Linux system is installed on hda5 partition and file system is reiserfs then we should issue a sequence of following commands:

```
# cd /tmp
# mkdir our_root_dir
# mount -t reiserfs /dev/hda5 our_root_dir
# chroot our_root_dir
```

Now, we can act the same way as if we were logged in into our Linux system. The final step is to install boot manager, which was wiped out by MS Windows. Should you decide to make it our

next step, follow the steps below accordingly to the boot manager
that we have installed - grub or lilo:

```
# update-grub

or

# lilo -v
```

Question 60: Preparation

How do I prepare for installation?

A: Linux makes more effective use of PC hardware than MS-DOS, Windows or NT, and is accordingly less tolerant of mis-configured hardware. There are few things you should do before you start so as to lessen your chances of being stopped by this kind of problem.

First step is to collect any manuals you have on your hardware; motherboard, video card, monitor, modem, etc., and have them within your reach.

Next step is to gather detailed information on your hardware configuration. One easy way to do this, if you're running MS-DOS 5.0, or up, is to print a report from the Microsoft diagnostic utility msd.exe (you can leave out the TSR, driver, memory-map, environment-strings and OS-version parts). This will guarantee you full and correct information on your video card and mouse type which will be helpful in configuring X later on.

Third, check your machine for configuration problems with supported hardware that could cause an un-recoverable lockup during Linux installation.

It is possible for a DOS/Windows system using IDE hard drive(s) and CD ROM to be functional even with the master/slave jumpers on the drives incorrectly set. Linux won't fly this way. If in doubt, check your master-slave jumpers.

If any of your peripheral hardware is designed with neither configuration jumpers nor non-volatile configuration memory, then it may require boot-time initialization via an MS-DOS utility to start up, and may not be easily accessible from Linux. CD-ROMs, sound cards, Ethernet cards and low-end tape drives can have this problem. If so, you may be able to work around this with an argument to the boot prompt; Google over Linux for details.

Some other operating systems will allow a bus mouse to share an IRQ with other devices. Linux doesn't support this, trying it may lock up your machine. I suggest for you to have thorough information on the bus mouse you are going to use.

Question 61: Linux Installation on Windows using Fips or Loadlin

How can I install Linux on a Windows partition as a disk image?

A: It is now possible to install Linux on a Windows partition as a disk image with what is known as the loopback filesystem. Red Hat and Mandrake offer this but it's an extremely bad idea because of the way Windows handles files. Defragging the system will become a nightmare and Linux itself will crawl and it will ruin both your Windows and Linux experience. The same applies to the Umsdos filesystem though Linux won't crawl and it's best to install Linux on a partition of its own. It is presumed that:

- You are using Windows 98 or higher.
- You are familiar with computers, at least you know how to boot the system using the floppy or CD ROM drive
- You know your way around DOS and Windows
- You know what a partition is and want to install Linux on a partition of its own
- You have a large hard disk – upward of 8.4 □ Gb – which currently holds Windows and on which you intend to install Linux (even those who with smaller disks can read on).

The first thing to do is to make space for Linux as you don't want to get stuck with a huge single partition with Windows on it. This would be your *C* drive. You have to make a separate partition for Linux out of this space (which would then be labeled as *D*). You can either use Windows Fdisk which really is not a good idea as it would entail losing all your data and making new partitions from scratch, one for Windows and one for Linux, or you can take the easier and far more convenient way out and use a free and excellent non-destructive partitioning utility called Fips. What makes Fips special is its ability to create a new partition out of the free space in your *C* partition without any loss of data. The latest version of Fips (2.0) is available at its homepage and most Linux distributions carry it under the /dostools or /dosutils directory in the primary cd.

We are going to concentrate on using Fips so if you are going to use Windows Fdisk, which actually is totally unnecessary unless you have just bought a new system and even then it's a better idea to make a single partition with Windows Fdisk, install Windows on it and then use Fips to split it for reasons that will be explained later.

A hard disk can have a maximum of 4 primary partitions. Apart from primary partitions a hard disk can also have what is known as an extended partition which in turn can hold a number of logical partitions. The extended partitions are not real partitions like primary or logical partitions in that they don't store data but are actually containers for logical partitions which is where data is actually stored. Thus in Windows, C: is a primary partition and if you used Windows Fdisk (Windows Fdisk will not make more than one primary partition to partition your hard disk) and D: is usually the first logical partition of the extended partition. E: would be the second logical partition and so on. In Linux things are slightly different. The first primary partition is called /dev/hda1, the second primary partition /dev/hda2 up to the fourth which is /dev/hda4. Linux refers to the an extended partition as in the case of a disk with 1 primary and one extended partition as /dev/hda1 for the primary and /dev/hda2 for the extended. The logical partitions of the extended partitions are referred to as /dev/hda5, /dev/hda6 and so on. The second hard disk would be referred to as /dev/hdb, the third /dev/hdc (usually the cdrom drive if set as secondary master) and the fourth and last hard disk as /dev/hdd (last because the motherboard has place for a maximum of 4 IDE devices). SCSI devices are referred to as /dev/sda.

Fips makes a new primary partition out of the free space in your hard disk. This is an inherently dangerous operation and it's a good idea to back up all your important data if something go wrong. Fips has been largely successful unless there is something already wrong with your hard disk.

Next step is for you to decide how you want to boot into Linux. The default and most common method is to use Lilo. It's a simple and basic bootloader program that overwrites (after saving) your hard disk's MBR (Master Boot Record) and on booting the system gives you a choice between booting either Windows or Linux. If you select Windows it boots Windows and you are met with the familiar windows screen or if you select Linux it boots Linux and if you don't make a choice in the stipulated time, it boots the default operating system, Windows or Linux, depending on how you set it up. You can restore your original MBR anytime, when uninstalling Linux for instance, either by typing /sbin/lilo -u within Linux or typing fdisk /MBR in DOS (this will overwrite the MBR with the original Windows MBR).

The problem with using Lilo especially for those with large disks is you would have to give up a substantial chunk of your disk space to Linux. This is not a flexible solution since while you can access your Windows partition from within Linux; the large MPEG files can be stored in Windows and accessed by both operating systems. Do know that BIOS cannot access data that is beyond this 1024 cylinder limit and Lilo is dependent on the BIOS to boot the OS. So if you want to use Lilo to boot Linux, make sure that the Linux partition is well below the 1024 cylinder limit. Most modern hard disks have more than 1024 cylinders and using Lilo means making the Linux partition at about the 1000 or 1010 cylinder mark which translates into a whopping 5.2 Gb of 12.9 Gb to Linux.

An underrated alternative to Lilo is to use Loadlin, especially for those with large hard-disks. It's an excellent alternative as you don't have to worry about the 1024 cylinder limit. Even better you can launch Linux from your Windows desktop and modify your autoexec.bat file to give you an option to boot into either of the OS's during boot time not unlike Lilo. You are then free to size your partitions as you please. For example, a 2.2 Gb extended partition with 3 logical partitions. It's normal to make three partitions, one for the Kernel boot files, one for the root partition and one for the swap partition.

Now we are ready to actually partition the hard disk. First make a DOS boot disk (type format a: /s at the DOS prompt or in DOS). Put the following three files in the disk, fips.exe, restorrb.exe and errors.txt. Defrag your hard disk; this puts all the data at the beginning leaving enough space for Fips to create a new partition from. If you use Norton Speed Disk, select the un-fragmented free space option. Norton usually puts data at the end of the disk and this will prevent Fips from creating a new partition. Run Scandisk and reboot using the boot disk you just created.

Type fips at the prompt and Fips will show you your partition table with a warning about partition table inconsistency. If your disk has more than 1024 cylinders it's usually safe to ignore this warning. Next Fips will ask you is you want to proceed, the program is extremely detailed; answer yes and when prompted to save a backup of your partition table and boot sector answer yes. This step is absolutely vital as it allows you to restore your hard disk to its un-partitioned single partition state should anything go wrong. It also comes in handy if you want to uninstall Linux or resize your Linux partition. It doesn't matter what happens to the new partition in the meantime, if you have the back up you can restore your hard disk to its original un-partitioned state. This reversible operation will work in all circumstances but one; if you format your original (Windows) partition which was split to make space for Linux in the meantime, the original FAT is overwritten with a new and smaller one and the restore operation will not work.

After making the backup you will be presented with a screen with 3 numbers, the first represents your original partition (it's the smallest size), Fips has allocated all free space in the hard disk to the new partition as this is the default behavior. The second column shows the cylinder info which will be the guide for those who plan to use Lilo. The third shows the size of the new partition you are going to create. Use the arrow keys to resize the partition; you would just have to reduce the size of the new partition since it is at its maximum to a size you want. For Lilo users, the new partition has to be below the 1024 cylinder mark, 1000 is a reasonable beginning for the new partition. After you are satisfied with the size of your new partition press enter, Fips will ask you to confirm and write the new partition table.

Reboot your system. Remember to change the BIOS settings to boot from the hard disk or you will end up rebooting with the floppy. Double click My Computer and you will see the result of all the hard work, there will be a new drive labeled D alongside the original C. Don't touch D, run scandisk on your original partition (C). If there are no errors, then you are ready to install Linux.

Some of the Linux documentation mistakenly asks you to delete the newly created partition using Windows Fdisk. Do not commit that mistake because if you do, the Linux partitions will show up in My Computer when you reboot after installing Linux and since Windows obviously cannot read these drives and the ext2 file system, using Explorer and accessing your hard disk in Windows will become a time consuming and tedious effort.

Reboot using your Linux Installation CD (let's focus on Redhat 6.2 which I find fairly straight forward). Most Linux distributions have really worked on their installation programs and you shouldn't have a problem. Just have the details about your hardware in hand, the horizontal and vertical refresh rate of your monitor in case the installation program doesn't automatically detect it (you will find the exact figures in the manual), the video card, its memory type (SDRAM or SGRAM) and size, and your mouse type – PS2 or Serial. As mentioned earlier, you will have to make about 3 partitions for Linux (3 is the recommended number). There are 3 main installation types, Workstation, Server and Custom. The Server class install erases everything in the hard disk so be careful. The workstation and custom installs have sub-classes but that's for you to explore.

Loadlin users have to select custom installation and dump Lilo when given the opportunity because the other types of installations install Lilo by default without asking. Lilo users have no restrictions; you can opt for whichever install type you like.

Lilo fans can use Disk Druid which is Red Hat's default partitioning utility. First, delete the second partition which will show up in Disk Druid's screen as /dev/hda2. Then create a new partition, set its mount point to /boot and size to 16 Mb. Create the second partition and set its mount point to / (that's called the root partition) and size to expandable. This tells Disk Druid to reclaim all free space after you have finished partitioning. Create the third partition and set its mount point to swap and size to about 127 Mb presuming you have 64 Mb RAM, those with less can make a 64 Mb swap partition.

Those who intend to use Loadlin however cannot use Disk Druid, they will have to use Linux Fdisk which may have an intimidating reputation but is actually pretty simple. When presented with the installation type screen select custom and with fdisk (you will find a small button with fdisk on it at the top of the screen). For some reason Disk Druid doesn't let you proceed with the installation if your /boot partition is above the 1024 cylinder limit, so if you try to use it to create the partitions, the install program will refuse to proceed. Fdisk is a pretty straight forward program and easy to use too. First you have to delete the partition you just created using Fips. Many people don't understand why they have to delete the partition they just created at considerable risk. This new partition is actually a FAT32 partition which Linux cannot use and when you delete it doesn't revert to being a part of C but is actually UNPARTITIONED FREE SPACE which you can use to create new partitions.

You have to understand a few Fdisk operations, typing m lists all the options, typing p at the prompt shows you the current partition table, d deletes a partition, n creates a partition, q quits without saving changes so if you make any mistakes there is nothing to worry about just type q and start all over again, w writes changes to the partition table use only after you are sure and L shows you the hex numbers for different partition types but you only need to know 2, Linux native is hex number 83 and Linux swap is hex number 82. While Disk Druid allows you to mount a swap partition without going into the hex numbers, in Fdisk the only way to make a swap partition is to give it its correct hex number which is 82.

Let's start, in Fdisk type p at the prompt and you will see the current partition table. Type d and select the partition you want to delete which in this case would be /dev/hda2 (just type 2) type p again and you will see the change reflected in the partition table. There will now be a single FAT32 partition /dev/hda1 (which is actually C). Type n to create a new partition and for type of partition the choices being primary or extended select e. There is no hard and fast rule about this. For instance, you could have a primary partition for /boot and an extended partition holding two logical partitions / and swap. I recommend an extended partition that holds three logical partitions. Now you have to size your extended partition properly since it's a container for the three logical partitions. From now on you just have to respond to Fdisk. It will ask you to set the size of the extended partition that you want to create. This partition will start where your Windows partition ends and ends at the end of the disk. You can either give the size in M (megabytes) in cylinder numbers or in K (kilobytes). Just accept the default for the start of the partition and select the end cylinder number for the end – Fdisk will give you the end cylinder number.

Repeat the operation for the three logical partitions, only this time you would have to select logical instead of extended and the appropriate sizes which are 16 Mb for the boot partition, 127 Mb for the swap partition (the size of the swap partition is variable depending on installed RAM, double your RAM is recommended) and the rest of the free space for the root (/) partition. After creating the three partitions type p and you will see the partitions you just created. There will be /dev/hda2 (extended) /dev/hda5 (logical) /dev/hda6 (logical) and /dev/hda7 (logical). There is just one thing left to do, set the hex number for the swap partition. Type t and select the 127 Mb partition you created which would be /dev/hda6 enter 6 for the partition number and 82 for the hex number (you will be prompted) and you have just finished with partitioning. Type w after making sure and Fdisk will write the new partition table and exit. The next screen will be the Disk Druid screen our Lilo friends have already seen and you just have to mount the partitions with Disk Druid. Select /dev/hda5 (the 16 Mb partition) and mount it as /boot. Select /dev/hda7 and mount it as / (the root partition)

The rest of the installation is straight forward. Select the packages you want, make the boot disk when given the opportunity to (absolutely essential especially for Loadlin users) and reboot the system. Lilo users should press dos at the Lilo prompt to boot into Windows. Lilo users should reboot the system and boot into Linux this time by typing linux at the Lilo prompt and depending on the choices you made you will either be at the console or the gnome or kde desktop. It's always a good idea to log into the console first and not graphically and then starting X because if X crashes, you can still have access to the system to make up for. Lilo is set to boot into Linux by default after a gap of 5 seconds, you can change the default to Windows by editing the lilo file in /etc. Look for the line that says default=linux and change it to dos. Alternative launch lilo from an xterm and change the asterisk from linux to dos (use the arrow buttons, dummy). That's set now for Lilo users.

Loadlin users still have a little work to do. First boot into Linux with the floppy. If you logged in graphically start a terminal emulator like xterm. There are always a couple of these under the utilities menu. Type mkdir /mnt/dosc. This is the first step to make your Windows partition accessible to Linux and this is particularly important for Loadlin users as it is the easiest way to transfer the Linux kernel to your Windows partition. Next start linuxconf from the system menu or the xterm and look for the filesystem menu. Expand access local drives and select add. Type /dev/hda1 in the partition field, vfat in the type field and /mnt/dosc/ in the mount point field and then mount the partition. Alternatively you can directly edit the fstab file in /etc in a text editor (Gedit is a good choice) and add the following line exactly as shown.

```
/dev/hda1     /mnt/dosc    vfat     defaults    0  0
```

This should give you access to your Windows partition, it will be in /mnt/dosc/. Copy the linux kernel to your C directory and rename it to vmlinuz. You will find it in /boot and probably called vmlinuz followed by your kernel version number. Do not copy the vmlinuz with an arrow in it, it's a symbolic link. Reboot into windows, get the loadlin package from the Linux cd, it will be in the /dostools/utils subdirectory. Unzip it and place Loadlin.exe in the C directory. Loadlin and the kernel can be anywhere on your windows partition but for the time being we will leave it in root directory of Windows. Now it's up to you how you want to boot into Linux. Read the loadlin documentation for the details. The roundabout way is to restart the system in DOS mode and type:

```
C:> loadlin vmlinuz root=/dev/hda7 ro
```

This will boot you into Linux. The easier way is to make a .bat file with the same information and placing it on your desktop. Open notepad type c:\loadlin c:\vmlinuz root=/dev/hda7 ro and save the file as linux.bat, right click the file, select advanced, and check the MS-DOS mode and warn settings. Make a shortcut to this file and put it on your desktop. The next time you want to boot into Linux just double click this file.

If you want to be prompted to boot into linux before Windows boots like the Lilo guys, you have to make another .bat file and call it from your autoexec.bat file. It's very simple and the details are available in the Loadlin documentation. The file looks a bit like this.

```
@echo off
cls
echo.
echo.
echo.
echo.
choice /t:n,5 "Do you wish to boot Linux?"
if errorlevel 2 goto End
c:\loadlin c:\vmlinuz  root=/dev/hda6  ro
End
```

Save this text as linux.bat or if there already is a linux.bat in your Windows root directory you can place it in another directory or give it another name. Add the following line to your autoexec.bat file c:\linux . The main thing if you are using a .bat file is to tell Loadlin where to find the kernel image file (vmlinuz). The above .bat file gives you the option to boot into Linux before Windows loads by typing y (for Linux) or n (for Windows) within five seconds at which point it boots Windows.

Question 62: Remove Linux and restore Windows partition

How do I remove Linux and restore Windows to its original state using Lilo or Loadlin?

A: Removing Linux depends whether you are using Lilo or Loadlin. Lilo users have to first restore their original MBR either by typing /sbin/lilo -u within Linux or typing fdisk /MBR in DOS. The next steps are common for both Loadlin and Lilo users. These are not really necessary but just to be on the safe side, try to do them.

Boot using the Linux installation CD and type Linux expert at the first prompt, answer whatever you wish to the next questions until you get to the install selection screen. Here, select Install and With Fdisk and use Fdisk to delete all Linux partitions. Write the changes to disk and Ctrl–Alt–Delete your way out of the installation program or reset your system to reboot. Remember to change the BIOS settings to boot from the hard disk or else you will reboot from the CDROM again.

Reboot once again, this time with the fips disk that has the backup of your partition table and boot sector and type restorrb at the prompt. Answer yes to the question, the program will restore your partition table and boot sector. Now you have reclaimed the lost partition space. This is the more reason for making sure that the crucial backup file (Rootboot.000) is saved in at least several different locations. It's better to be safe than sorry. Reboot back into Windows and run scandisk on the newly increased C drive. It will report one error in the fsinfo sector which is just a used and free space accounting error. Your Linux data is now naturally lost for ever. Hopefully this procedure won't be necessary unless you are increasing space allocated to Linux or getting rid of Windows.

Question 63: Choosing a package

Which package should I install?

A: Linux software comes in "packages". For example, Linux Mandrake 7.0 installation CD contained 1002 packages. Mandrake 7.2 packs 2 CDs of software will put 1123 packages on the hard drive. Mandrake tends to pack more software than RedHat.

No matter what distribution or version, the CD contains packages that make the base operating system (kernel, libraries, a selection of command-line configuration and maintenance tools, etc) a rich selection of networking "clients" and servers" with appropriate configuration and monitoring tools, some end-user text mode applications, base X-windowing system and at least one GUI desktop and it's applications.

The installation program (either RedHat or Mandrake) will ask you which packages to install. If you select "workstation installation", then the packages normally found on servers will be omitted from your. If you choose "server installation", then typically the end-user desktop applications will not be installed. You can also choose to install "everything" and this is a popular option for a home computer installation. If you are a newbie, it pays to trust the defaults selected by your distribution creator.

I suggest for you to stay away from the tempting installation option "expert install--select packages manually" unless you wish to install everything anyway. For starters, I like the safe "max default installation", however this installation option is called on your CD.

You can easily install a package that you may find need for it later.

Question 64: KDE or GNOME

Which GUI desktop should I install, KDE or GNOME?

A: If you have enough disk space, definitely install both. You can later decide if you prefer KDE, GNOME or another desktop but whatever your choice, you definitely want both the KDE and the GNOME libraries installed. Once you have the libraries installed, KDE programs can be run under GNOME and vice versa, which is great because there are nice applications written using either library. As far as the amount of disk space is concerned, the "desktop" is only a small part of the KDE and GNOME systems so you don't save much space by omitting the desktop and trying to install "libraries only". Both GNOME and KDE come with a set of nice programs and tools, so it is definitely worth it to install both desktops in full. I never heard that the two adversely interfered with each other. For every day work, use the KDE desktop because it feels more solid than GNOME.

You can also install the other "alternative windows managers". They hardly take any space and can be useful under some situation. You can run any KDE or GNOME application from under any of them as long as KDE and GNOME libraries are installed.

KDE is more power hungry. On older hardware (e.g., 133 MHz Pentium), GNOME is preferable to KDE. Other windows managers are lighter than either KDE or GNOME. Hence on a really modest hardware, choose one of the "alternative" windows managers.

Question 65: Log-in as root

I finished the installation. How do I log-in for the very first time?

A: Log-in as root. "root" is the only account that exists after the initial installation (newer installation programs do prompt you to create a regular user account during the installation). Example text mode login:

```
my_machine_name login: root
Password:  my_password
```

In the example above, I typed the word "root" at the login prompt. After that, I entered the password that I chose during the initial Linux installation. The password did not appear on the screen when I typed it (for security reasons). After I login, I find myself in a text-mode terminal.

If you installed the GUI login screen, the login procedure looks similar but occurs on an X-window screen (if you occasionally have problems typing there, perhaps remember that your mouse cursor must be above the dialog box. The X login screen implements the "focus-follows-mouse" policy). After a successful login, my default GUI desktop is launched.

"root" is a special account with an absolute power over the system, and it is used for system administration. You surely want to create at least one more "user" account later to do regular work.

Chapter V: Devices, Linux File Systems, File System Hierarchy Standard

Question 66: The root file system

What are the characteristics of a root file system? How does it function?

A: The root filesystem should generally be small, since it contains very critical files and a small, infrequently modified filesystem has a better chance of not getting corrupted. A corrupted root filesystem will generally mean that the system becomes unbootable except with special measures (e.g., from a floppy), so you don't want to risk it.

The root directory generally doesn't contain any files, except perhaps on older systems where the standard boot image for the system, usually called /vmlinuz was kept there. (Most distributions have moved those files the /boot directory. Otherwise, all files are kept in subdirectories under the root filesystem:

/bin - Commands needed during bootup that might be used by normal users (probably after bootup).

/sbin - Like /bin, but the commands are not intended for normal users, although they may use them if necessary and allowed. /sbin is not usually in the default path of normal users, but will be in root's default path.

/etc - Configuration files specific to the machine.

/root - The home directory for user root. This is usually not accessible to other users on the system

/lib - Shared libraries needed by the programs on the root filesystem.

/lib/modules - Loadable kernel modules, especially those that are needed to boot the system when recovering from disasters (e.g., network and filesystem drivers).

/dev - Device files. These are special files that help the user interface with the various devices on the system.

/tmp - Temporary files. As the name suggests, programs running often store temporary files in here.

/boot - Files used by the bootstrap loader, e.g., LILO or GRUB. Kernel images are often kept here instead of in the root directory. If there are many kernel images, the directory can easily grow rather big, and it might be better to keep it in a separate filesystem. Another reason would be to make sure the kernel images are within the first 1024 cylinders of an IDE disk. This 1024 cylinder limit is no longer true in most cases. With modern BIOS and later versions of LILO (the Linux Loader) the 1024 cylinder limit can be passed with logical block addressing (LBA). See the lilo manual page for more details.

/mnt - Mount point for temporary mounts by the system administrator. Programs aren't supposed to mount on /mnt automatically. /mnt might be divided into subdirectories (e.g., /mnt/dosa might be the floppy drive using an MS-DOS filesystem, and /mnt/exta might be the same with an ext2 filesystem).

/proc, /usr, /var, /home - Mount points for the other filesystems. Although /proc does not reside on any disk in reality it is still mentioned here.

Question 67: files on Linux

How does Linux treat file names? What are hidden files and directories?

A: Always keep in mind that file names are case sensitive. This means that PFile isn't the same thing as pfile or PFILE.

Linux doesn't use file name extensions like MS Windows does. You can name all your files the way you want because the type and purpose of the file are determined in different ways. Surely you can use file name extensions if it helps you determine faster what type your files are and it's a good practice to use the extensions.

There are more files on your system than you can see, these are hidden files. For example, change to your home directory and list the contents of it with ls. You see some files and directories there but you don't see all of them because some files are hidden. The -a option is used when you want to display all files and that includes hidden ones: $ ls -a

When a file name starts with a dot, it's a hidden file and you don't see it when you do a normal directory listing. Directories can also be hidden the same way; put a dot in front of the directory name and you won't see the directory or its contents when you do a normal directory listing.

Usually these hidden files are configuration files and most of them were placed into your home directory when your user account was created. They're used for configuring different things related to your account and some apps also store their configuration and setting files in your home directory as hidden files or in hidden directories. It is an advantage to hide configuration files because they won't muddle up your home directory and so you'll find the rest of your files more easily.

Question 68: Linux file system

How do I move around the Linux file system?

A: The files on Linux system are arranged in a hierarchal directory structure like in MS Windows. This means that the files are organized in a tree-like pattern of directories (or folders in windows). Those directories may contain files or other directories, which in turn may contain more files or directories and so on.

On a Linux system, all the files and directories are under the very same tree unlike in Windows. The first directory in this system, the one where the tree starts from, is called the root directory. Everything, every single file and directory on a Linux system, is under this root directory.

Like in a graphical file manager, you're always working in a single directory when you're at the CLI, and the directory can be anywhere in the file system tree. The directory contains files and a way to go to its parent directory and its subdirectories. The directory where you're currently working in, is called the working directory. To find out where the working directory is, use the pwd command that stands for print working directory. Now type it and see where you are.

```
you@puter: ~$ pwd
/home/you
you@puter: ~$
```

You will be in your home directory now. This is where you put your personal files and usually the working directory is set to your home directory when you log in to your Linux system. The home directories of users are located under /home and usually the name of your home directory is /home/your_user_name.

Now that you know where you are, try to know what there is. For finding it out, type the ls command. You will get a list of all the files and subdirectories that your working directory contains.

You have a way of controlling what the ls command displays and how. Just like almost every Linux command, ls can have additional options that change the behavior of it. For example, try typing this: **you@puter: ~$ ls -l**

You will get again a list of the files in your working directory but the output of ls is now different with the -l option. You get additional info about the files your directory contains. This option told ls to display more information about the files in the current directory. These additions to commands are often called parameters or arguments or options. So in this case, ls was the command and -l was the option.

You can separate the command from its options with a space and you can also add more options and separate them from each other with a space as well. For example, the -r option tells ls to display the files in reverse order. If you want to display both the files in reverse order and get more info about the files, you could do it with: **you@puter: ~$ ls -l -r**

In some cases, you can use a shorter form when using multiple options. The following does the same thing: you@puter: ~$ ls -lr

Many commands accept a lot of arguments and some commands also accept file or directory names as arguments. For example, when you give the ls command without any arguments, it displays the contents of the current directory. If you want to display the contents of some other directory, you can give the pathname of the desired directory as an argument to ls. A pathname is the path you take along the directories to the destination directory. There are two kinds of pathnames; absolute pathnames and relative pathnames.

An absolute pathname simply tells you what the complete path to a certain file or directory is. Because all the files on Linux are under the root directory, an absolute pathname must start from the root directory and then follow the filesystem tree directory by directory until you get to the desired file or directory.

All absolute file names start with a slash because the slash indicates the root directory. For example, there's a directory called /usr/X11R6/bin on your system. The path here means that you start from the root directory (/), go to its subdirectory "usr", which contains a directory called "X11R6", which in turn contains the "bin" directory. As you noticed, you use the slash not only for indicating the root directory but also for separating the directories on the path. This is different from Windows where you use a backslash for separating the directories.

To change the working directory, use the cd command and give the desired directory as an argument to it. Now, change your working directory to /usr/X11R6: me@puter: ~$ cd /usr/X11R6

Now check if your new working directory really is what you wanted:

```
you@puter:  /usr/X11R6$ pwd
/usr/X11R6
you@puter:  /usr/X11R6$
```

Take note that the command prompt has changed. Usually it's configured to display the name of the working directory. Now you don't have to type pwd all the time.

You already know that an absolute pathname starts from the root directory. However, a relative pathname starts from the working directory. This is why you need some special symbols for indicating the relative positions in the filesystem. These symbols are a dot (.) and two dots (..) and they mean the working directory and the parent directory, respectively.

Let's see how these things work. Now your current working directory should be /usr/X11R6. List the contents of it:

```
you@puter:  /usr/X11R6$ ls
bin include lib man
you@puter:  /usr/X11R6$
```

There should be a directory called "lib" and you want to find out what it contains but you don't want to change the working directory. There are two ways of doing this. Use the absolute pathname: you@puter: /usr/X11R6$ ls /usr/X11R6/lib

Or use the relative pathname: you@puter: /usr/X11R6$ ls ./lib

Here, the dot in the path ./lib refers to the working directory which is /usr/X11R6. You will save some more typing if you omit the leading dot. In most cases you don't need it, so this would've been the same as the above: you@puter: /usr/X11R6$ ls lib Now let's change the working directory to /usr/X11R6/bin. There are also two ways of doing this. You can use absolute pathname:
you@puter: /usr/X11R6$ cd /usr/X11R6/bin

Or use relative pathname (omit the dot): you@puter:
/usr/X11R6$ cd bin

Now your current working directory is /usr/X11R6/bin. To change it to /usr/X11R6 which is the parent directory, use the absolute pathname: you@puter: /usr/X11R6/bin$ cd /usr/X11R6

However, it's faster to use the two dots (parent directory):
you@puter: /usr/X11R6/bin$ cd ..

Note the space between cd and the dots. In many cases using relative pathnames instead of absolute ones saves some typing.

Question 69: Determine the type of a file

How do I determine the type of an unfamiliar file on the Linux system?

A: If you see a strange file on your system and don't know what it is, it's often helpful to determine its type. If the file has a file name extension, you probably can determine its type easily, but if you don't recognize the extension or if the file doesn't have one, you need different ways of finding out what sort of a file it is. This is where the file command comes in handy. The file command examines a file's contents and tells you what kind of a file it is:

```
you@puter: ~$ file examine.html
examine.html: HTML document text
you@puter: ~$
```

You can also give multiple files as arguments to file, if you want:

```
you@puter: ~$ file view_this picture.gif
view_this: ASCII English text
picture.gif: GIF image data, version 89a, 88 x 31
you@puter: ~$
```

Just give the file name as an argument to file and then it tells you the type of the file and maybe some additional information about it.

Question 70: Permissions and ownership

I'm the only user in my Linux and I cannot access some of my files.

Have I mis-configured file access permissions?

A: Linux is designed to be a multi-user environment. It is necessary to have a secure system for deciding which files are yours and who can fiddle with them. Even if you're the only user on an ordinary desktop system, file permissions helps you keep your important files safe from outsiders.

Every file on your Linux system, including directories, is owned by a specific user and group. Therefore, file permissions are defined separately for users, groups, and others.

User: The username of the person who owns the file. By default, the user who creates the file will become its owner.

Group: The usergroup that owns the file. All users who belong into the group that owns the file will have the same access permissions to the file. This is useful if, for example, you have a project that requires a bunch of different users to be able to access certain files, while others can't. In that case, you'll add all the users into the same group, make sure the required files are owned by that group and set the file's group permissions accordingly.

Other: A user who isn't the owner of the file and doesn't belong in the same group the file does. Hence, if you set permission for the "other" category, it will affect everyone else by default. For this reason, people often talk about setting the "world" permission bit when they mean setting the permissions for "other."

There are three types of access permissions on Linux: read, write, and execute. These permissions are defined separately for the file's owner, group and all other users.

Read permission: On a regular file, the read permission bit means the file can be opened and read. On a directory, the read permission means you can list the contents of the directory.

Write permission: On a regular file, this means you can modify the file or write new data to the file. In the case of a directory, the write permission means you can add, remove, and rename files in the directory. This means that if a file has the write permission bit, you are allowed to modify the file's contents, but you're allowed to rename or delete the file only if the permissions of the file's directory allow you to do so.

Execute permission: In the case of a regular file, this means you can execute the file as a program or a shell script. On a directory, the execute permission allows you to access files in the directory. Although the execute bit lets you enter the directory, you're not allowed to list its contents unless you also have the read permissions to that directory.

Question 71: View file permissions

How can I view file permissions?

A: You can view the access permissions of a file by doing the long directory listing with the ls -l command. For example, it may look like this:

```
you@puter: /home/writers$ ls -l
total 10
drwxr-xr-x 3   dan writers 180 2005-10-05 21:37
dir

-rw-r-----     2   dan writers 818 2005-09-04 13:35
file

-rwxr-xr-x  1   dan writers 1348 2005-08-03 20:31
otherfile
```

The very first column shows the file type and permissions. The second column shows the number of links or directory entries that refer to the file, the third shows the owner of the file and the fourth one shows the group the file belongs to. The other columns show the file's size in bytes, date and time of last modification and the filename.

The first column shows the files' permissions is arranged into four separate groups. The first group consists of only one character and it shows the file's type. For example, d means a directory and - means a normal file, so if you take a look at our example output, you'll notice dir is a directory while file and otherfile are regular files.

The first character can be any of these:

d = directory
- = regular file
l = symbolic link
s = Unix domain socket
p = named pipe
c = character device file

b = block device file

The next nine characters show the file's permissions, divided into three groups, each consisting of three characters. The first group of three characters shows the read, write, and execute permissions for user, the owner of the file. The next group shows the read, write, and execute permissions for the group of the file. Similarly, the last group of three characters shows the permissions for other, everyone else. In each group, the first character means the read permission, the second one write permission, and the third one executes permission.

The characters are pretty easy to remember.

r = read permission
w = write permission
x = execute permission
- = no permission

Now let's go back to our sample output above. You already know that dir is a directory, because the first column begins with a d. The owner of this directory is user dan and the group owner is writers. The first three characters, rwx, indicate the directory's owner, dan in this case, has full access to the directory. The user dan is able to access, view, and modify the files in that directory. The next three characters, r-x, indicate that all users belonging to group writers have read and execute permissions to the directory. They can change into the directory, execute files, and view its contents. However, because they don't have write permissions, they can't make any changes to the directory content. Finally, the last three characters, r-x, indicate that all the users who are not dan or don't belong into group writers, have read and execute permissions in the directory.

Also, the first column that begins with a (-) is a regular file, owned by user dan and group writers, just like the directory in our example. The first three characters, rw-, indicate the owner has read and write access to the file. According to the next three characters, r--, the users belonging to group writers can view the file but not modify or execute it. The final three characters, ---, indicate no one else has any access to the file.

Similarly, you can see otherfile is a regular file and its owner has full access to it, while everyone else can read and execute the file but not modify it.

Question 72: file permissions in symbolic mode

Can the root user and the file's owner set file permissions?

A: The root user and the file's owner can set file permissions. It is done with the chmod command. Chmod has two modes – symbolic and numeric.

The symbolic mode is easy to perform. First, you decide if you set permissions for the user (u), the group (g), others (o), or all of the three (a). Then, you either add a permission (+), remove it (-), or wipe out the previous permissions and add a new one (=). Next, you decide if you set the read permission (r), write permission (w), or execute permission (x). Lastly, you'll tell chmod which file's permissions you want to change.

Suppose we have a regular file called redfile, and the file has full access permissions for all the groups (long directory listing would show -rwxrwxrwx as the file's permissions).

Wipe out all the permissions but add read permission for everybody:
```
$ chmod a=r redfile
```
After the command, the file's permissions would be -r--r--r--

Add execute permissions for group:
```
$ chmod g+x redfile
```
Now, the file's permissions would be -r--r-xr--

Add both write and execute permissions for the file's owner. Note how you can set more than one permission at the same time:
```
$ chmod u+wx redfile
```
After this, the file permissions will be -rwxr-xr--

Remove the execute permission from both the file's owner and group. Note, again, how you can set them both at once:
```
$ chmod ug-x redfile
```
Now, the permissions are -rw-r--r--

The following is the summary for setting file permissions in symbolic mode:

Which user?
u   user/owner
g   group
o   other
a   all

What to do?
+   add this permission
-      remove this permission
=   set exactly this permission

Which permissions?
r   read
w   write
x   execute

Question 73: set file permissions in numeric mode

Now that I know how to set file permissions in symbolic mode, how about in numeric mode?

A: In the numeric mode, the file permissions aren't represented by characters. Instead, they are represented by a three-digit octal number.

4 = read (r)
2 = write (w)
1 = execute (x)
0 = no permission (-)

To get the permission bits you want, you add up the numbers accordingly. For example, the rwx permissions would be 4+2+1=7, rx would be 4+1=5, and rw would be 4+2=6. Because you set separate permissions for the owner, group, and others, you'll need a three-digit number representing the permissions of all these groups.

Here's an example:
```
$ chmod 755 redfile
```
This would change the redfile's permissions to -rwxr-xr-x. The owner would have full read, write, and execute permissions (7=4+2+1), the group would have read and execute permissions (5=4+1), and the world would have the read and execute permissions as well.

Let's have another example:
```
$ chmod 640 redfile
```
In this case, redfile's permissions would be -rw-r-----. The owner would have read and write permissions (6=4+2), the group would have read permissions only (4), and the others wouldn't have any access permissions (0).

The numeric mode may not be as straightforward as the symbolic mode, but with the numeric mode, you can more quickly and efficiently set the file permissions.

Here is a quick reference for setting file permissions in numeric mode:

Which number?

0	---
1	--x
2	-w-
3	-wx
4	r--
5	r-x
6	rw-
7	rwx

Question 74: Change file and group ownership

How can I change a file's owner and group in Linux?

A: You can change the owner and group ownership of files and directories with the chown and chgrp commands.

1. Use of chown:
You can change the owner and group of a file or a directory with the chown command if you are the root user or the owner of the file.

Set the file's owner:
```
$ chown clark   redfile
```
After giving this command, the new owner of a file called redfile will be the user clark. The file's group owner will not change. Instead of a user name, you can also give the user's numeric ID here if you want.

You can also set the file's group at the same time. If the user name is followed by a colon and a group name, the file's group will be changed as well.
```
$ chown clark:clarkgroup somefile
```
After giving this command, redfile's new owner would be user clark and the group clarkgroup.

You can set the owner of a directory exactly the same way you set the owner of a file:
```
$ chown username somedir
```
Note that after giving this command, only the owner of the directory will change. The owner of the files inside of the directory won't change.

In order to set the ownership of a directory and all the files in that directory, you'll need the -R option:
```
$ chown -R username somedir
```
Here, R stands for recursive because this command will recursively change the ownership of directories and their contents. After issuing this example command, the user

username will be the owner of the directory somedir, as well as every file in that directory.

```
If: $ chown -v username somefile
changed ownership of 'somefile' to username
```

Here, v stands for verbose. If you use the -v option, chown will list what it did (or didn't do) to the file.

The verbose mode is especially useful if you change the ownership of several files at once. For example, this could happen when you do it recursively:

```
$ chown -Rv username somedir
changed ownership of 'somedir/' to username
changed ownership of 'somedir/bluefile' to username
changed ownership of 'somedir/redfile' to username
```

As you can see, chown nicely reports to you what it did to each file.

2. Use of chgrp: change the group ownership of a file.
You can also use the chgrp command to change the group of a file or a directory. Also as with chown, you must be either the root user or the owner of the file in order to change the group ownership.

The command chgrp works pretty much the same way as chown does, except it changes the file's user group instead of the owner.
```
$ chgrp usergroup redfile
```
After issuing this command, the file redfile will be owned by a user group usergroup. Although the file's group has changed to usergroup, the file's owner will still be the same.

The options of using chgrp are the same as using chown. So, for example, the -R and -v options will work with it just like they worked with chown:
```
$ chgrp -Rv usergroup somedir
changed group of 'somedir/' to usergroup
changed group of 'somedir/bluefile' to usergroup
changed group of 'somedir/redfile' to usergroup
```

The command chown nicely reports to you what it did to each file.

Question 75: View text files

I want to see or read the files in my Linux file system. What command do I use?

A: You can view and edit text files with cat and less.

The "cat" is a simple little program that displays the contents of a text file when you give the file name as an argument to it: $ cat view_this

This is a nice way of viewing short files that fit on your screen. If the file is long and its contents cannot be displayed on your screen all at once, use less instead.

The "less" is a program that lets you view long text files. You use less by giving the file name as an argument to it: $ less view_this

When viewing the file, you can use Page Up and Page Down keys to move through the file and typing q will exit.

It is also possible to open several files at the same time so you can navigate from one file to next without closing it first. If you want to open several files, just give all the file names at once: $ less file1 file2 file3

When viewing several files at the same time, you can use :n for examining the next file and :p for the previous file.

Here are some widely used commands in less:

Command / key	Action
e, j, Down, or Enter	move forward one line
y, k, or Up	move backward one line
f, Space, or Page Down	move forward one page
b, or Page Up	move backward one page

/characters	search forward in the file for lines containing the
n	repeat the previous search
:e file_name	examine a new file
:n	examine the next file
:p	examine the previous file
h, or ?	display help
q	quit

Question 76: File manipulation mv command

I have already created a directory for my files, how can I clean up my unclassified files?

A: The mv command can be used for moving or renaming files. To rename a file, you can use it like this:

```
$ mv file file2
```

If file2 doesn't exist, it'll be created but if it exists, it'll be overwritten. If you want to be prompted before overwriting files, you can use the -i option the same way as with cp:

```
$ mv -i file file2
mv: overwrite `file2'? y
$
```

To move the file into another directory:

```
$ mv file dir1
```

If you want to rename the file to file2 and move it into another directory:

```
$ mv file dir1/file2
```

Detailed information about the syntax and features of the mv command can be found in the man or Info pages. The use of this documentation should always be your first reflex when confronted with a problem. Even experienced users read man pages every day, so beginning users should read them all the time. After a while, you will get to know the most common options to the common commands, but you will still need the documentation as a primary source of information.

Question 77: File manipulation cp command

How can I copy files?

A: You can use the cp command to copy files. The following will copy file to file2. Note that if file2 doesn't exist, it'll be created but if it exists, it'll be overwritten:

$ cp file file2

There is no undo command in the Linux CLI, so be very carefull to as you might accidentally overwrite an important file. The risk of doing so is smaller if you use the -i option ("interactive") with cp. The following does the same as the above, but if file2 exists, you'll be prompted before overwriting:

$ cp -i file file2
cp: overwrite `file2'? n
$

It's a best use the -i option whenever you're dealing with important files.

If you want to copy file into directory dir1:

$ cp file dir1

The following would do the same as the above, copy file into dir1, but under a different name:

$ cp file dir1/file2

You can also copy multiple files into one directory with a single command:

$ cp file1 file2 file3 dir1

Note that if the last argument isn't a directory name, you'll get an error message complaining about it.

Question 78: File manipulation rm command

How can I remove files or directories?

A: The rm command is used for removing files and directories. To remove a file:

$ rm file

You can also delete more files at once:

rm file1 file2

To remind you again, Linux doesn't have any undo commands and it doesn't put files into Trash where you can save them later. Once you've deleted a file, it's forever gone unless you have back-ups. To protect beginners from "damage", the interactive behavior of the rm, cp and mv commands can be activated using the -i option. In this case, the system won't immediately act upon request. Instead it will ask for confirmation, so it takes an additional click on the enter key to inflict the damage: Here's an example:

```
jim:~> rm -ri archive/
rm: descend into directory `archive'? y
rm: descend into directory `archive/reports'? y
rm: remove directory `archive/reports'? y
rm: descend into directory `archive/backup'? y
rm: remove `archive/backup/sysbup200112.tar'? y
rm: remove directory `archive/backup'? y
rm: remove directory `archive'? y
```

Question 79: Creating a directory

I want to create directories and subdirectories for my files. How can I do this?

A: That can be done with the mkdir command:

```
jim:~> mkdir archive

jim:~> ls -ld archive
drwxrwxrwx  2 jim jim        1111  Jan 11 11: 11 archive/
```

If you want to create directories and subdirectories in one step, this can be done using the -p option:

```
jim:~> cd archive

jim:~/archive> mkdir 20004 20005 20006

richard:~/archive> ls
2004/  2005/  2006/

richard:~/archive> mkdir 2004/reports/Books/
mkdir: cannot create directory `2004/reports/Books/':
No such file or directory

jim:~/archive> mkdir -p 2004/reports/Books/

richard:~/archive> ls 2004/reports
/Books/
```

If the new file needs other permissions than the default file creation permissions, the new access rights can be set in one move, still using the mkdir command.

The name of a directory has to comply with the same rules as those applied on regular file names. One of the most important restrictions is that you can't have two files with the same name in one directory. There are virtually no limits on the length of a file name, but it is usually kept shorter than 80 characters, so it can fit on one line of a terminal. You can use any character you want in a file name, although it is advised to exclude characters that have a special meaning to the shell.

Question 80: Remove directories

I want to remove empty directories. What is the best way to do this?

A: There are two commands you can use for removing directories. If the directory is empty, you can use rmdir:

```
$ rmdir dir1
```

If you want to remove a directory with all its contents, you can use rm with the -r option. The -r option tells rm to remove a directory recursively:

```
$ rm -r dir1
```

It is best to use the -i option when deleting a directory with its contents so that you'd be prompted before each file in the directory.

```
$ rm -ir dir1
```

Question 81: Copy and move directories

How do I copy and move selected directories in Linux?

A: For copying and moving directories you can use the cp and mv commands just like you use them with files. You've probably noticed that cp just complains at you if you've already tried to copy a directory with cp. The cp command wants you to use the -r option if you want to copy a directory with its contents. The -r means "copy recursively":

```
$ cp -r dir1 dir2
```

The above creates a directory named dir2 whose contents will be identical to dir1. However, if dir2 already exists, nothing will be overwritten: the directory dir1 will be copied into the dir2 directory under the name dir2/dir1.

When renaming directories, use the mv command exactly the same way as with files:

```
$ mv dir1 dir2
```

When dealing with directories, mv works a bit like cp does. If dir2 doesn't exist, the above will rename dir1 to dir2, but if dir2 exists, the directory dir1 will be moved into the dir2 directory under the name dir2/dir1.

Question 82: df command

What tool can I use to view disk usage?

A: The primary tools for getting information about files and file systems are all relatively simple and easy to use. df (shows disk usage) will also show inode usage, df –i (inodes contain information about files such as their location on the disk drive, and you can run out of these before you run out of disk space if you have many small files. This results in error messages of "disk full" when in fact "df" will show there is free space ("df –i" however would show the inodes are all used). This is similar to file allocation entries in Windows, with vfat it actually stores names in 8.3 formats, using multiple entries for long filenames, with a maximum of 512 entries per directory, to many long filenames, and the directory is 'full'.

Simply type in df and you'll be shown disk usage for all your mounted file systems in 1K blocks. For example:

```
user@server:~> df
Filesystem    1K-blocks     Used    Available  Use%  Mounted on
/dev/hda3      5242904    759692     4483212  1  5%  /
tmpfs           127876      8001       27868     1%  /dev/shm
/dev/hda1       127351     33047       87729    28%  /boot
/dev/hda9     10485816     33508    10452308     1%  /home
/dev/hda8      5242904    932468     4310436    18%  /srv
/dev/hda7      3145816     32964     3112852     2%  /tmp
/dev/hda5      5160416    474336     4423928    10%  /usr
/dev/hda6      3145816    412132     2733684    14%  /var
```

Question 83: fsck command

How do I check and repair files for inconsistencies?

A: The fsck command ("file system check" or "file system consistency check") is a tool for checking the consistency of a file system. The file system can become inconsistent due to several reasons and the most common is abnormal shutdown due to hardware failure, power failure or switching off the system without proper shutdown. Due to these reasons, the super block in a file system is not updated and has mismatched information relating to system data blocks, free blocks and inodes .

Typically, fsck utilities provide options for interactively repairing damaged file systems (the user must decide how to fix specific problems), allowing fsck to decide how to fix specific problems or reviewing the problems that need to be resolved without actually fixing them.

Fsck can also be run manually by the system administrator if there is believed to be a problem with the file system.

Modes of operation: fsck operates in two modes interactive and non-interactive:

interactive : the fsck examines the file system and stops at each error it finds in the file system and gives the problem description and ask for user response usually whether to correct the problem or continue without making any change to the file system.

Non-interactive :fsck tries to repair all the problems it finds in a file system without stopping for user response useful in case of a large number of inconsistencies in a file system but has the disadvantage of removing some useful files which are detected to be corrupt .

If file system is found to have problem at the booting time non interactive fsck is run and all errors which are considered safe to correct are corrected. But if still file system has problems the system boots in single user mode asking for user to manually run the fsck to correct the problems in file system fsck should always be run in a single user mode which ensures proper repair of file system. If it is run in a busy system where the file system is changing constantly fsck may see the changes as inconsistencies and may corrupt the file system.

If the system can not be brought in a single user mode, fsck should be run on the partitions, other than root & usr , after unmounting them. Root & usr partitions can not be unmounted. If the system fails to come up due to root/usr files system corruption, the system can booted with CD and root/usr partitions can be repaired using fsck.

Command syntax:

```
fsck   [ -F fstype]   [-V]      [-yY]      [-o options]
special
```

-F fstype   type of file system to be repaired (ufs , vxfs etc)

-V verify the command line syntax but do not run the command

-y or -Y Run the command in non interactive mode - repair all errors encountered without waiting for user response.

-o options Three options can be specified with -o flag

b=n   where n is the number of next super block if primary super block is corrupted in a file system.

The p option is used to make safe repair options during the booting process.

"f" forces the file system check regardless of its clean flag.

"special" - Block or character device name of the file system to be checked/repaired - for example /dev/rdsk/cot3dos4. Character device should be used for consistencies check & repair

Phases:

fsck checks the file system in a series of 5 pages and checks a specific functionality of file system in each phase.

Phase 1 - Check Blocks and Sizes

Phase 2 - Check Pathnames

Phase 3 - Check Connectivity

Phase 4 - Check Reference Counts

Phase 5 - Check Cylinder Groups

Error messages & corrective action:

1. Corrupted superblock - fsck fails to run
If the superblock is corrupted the file system still can be repaired using alternate superblock which are formed while making new file system .

The first alternate superblock number is 32 and others superblock numbers can be found using the following command:

```
newfs -N /dev/rdsk/c0t0d0s6
```

For example, to run fsck using first alternate superblock following command is used:

```
fsck -F ufs -o b=32 /dev/rdsk/c0t0d0s6
```

2. Link counter adjustment: fsck finds mismatch between directory inode link counts and actual directory links and prompts for adjustment in case of interactive operation. Link count adjustments are considered to be a safe operation in a file system and should be repaired by giving 'y' response to the "adjust?" prompt during fsck.

3. Free Block count salvage: During fsck the number of free blocks listed in a super block and actual unallocated free blocks count does not match. fsck inform this mismatch and asks to salvage free block count to synchronize the superblock count. This error can be corrected without any potential problem to the file system or files.

4. Unreferenced file reconnection: While checking connectivity fsck finds some inodes which are allocated but not referenced - not attached to any directory. Answering y to reconnect message by fsck links these files to the lost+found directory with their inode number as their name.

To get more info about the files in lost+found 'file' command can be used to see the type of files and subsequently they can be opened in their applications or text editors to find out about their contents. If the file is found to be correct it can be used after copying to some other directory and renaming it.

Question 84: du command

What does the du command do?

A: To view usage by a directory or file you can use du. Unless you specify a filename, du will act recursively. For example:

```
user@server:~> du file.txt
1300    file.txt
```

Unless you specify a filename du will act recursively.

```
user@server:~> du -h /usr/local
4.0K    /usr/local/games
16K     /usr/local/include/nessus/net
180K    /usr/local/include/nessus
208K    /usr/local/include
62M     /usr/local/lib/nessus/plugins/.desc
97M     /usr/local/lib/nessus/plugins
164K    /usr/local/lib/nessus/plugins_factory
97M     /usr/local/lib/nessus
12K     /usr/local/lib/pkgconfig
2.7M    /usr/local/lib/ladspa
104M    /usr/local/lib
112K    /usr/local/man/man1
4.0K    /usr/local/man/man2
4.0K    /usr/local/man/man3
4.0K    /usr/local/man/man4
16K     /usr/local/man/man5
4.0K    /usr/local/man/man
```

If you just want a summary of that directory you can use the -s option.

```
user@server:~> du -hs /usr/local
210M    /usr/local
```

Question 85: Mounting files

I'm migrating to Linux from Microsoft Windows. I inserted my floppy and CD into the drive and I was not able to access it.

Why did this happen?

A: If you're migrating to Linux from Microsoft Windows, you're probably used to accessing all your file systems very easily. However, this isn't the case in Linux. Your floppies, CDs, hard disk partitions and other storage devices must be attached to some existing directory on your system before they can be accessed. This attaching is called mounting and the directory where the device is attached is called a mount point.

After the device is mounted, you can access the files on that device by accessing the directory where the device is attached. When you're done and want to remove the floppy or CD or other device, you need to detach, unmount it before removing it.

Mounting is done with the mount command.

When mounting, you must tell the mount command what is the device or partition you want to mount and what is the mount point. The mount point must be a directory that already exists on your system. For example, to mount your floppy:

```
$ mount /dev/fd0 /mnt/floppy
```

In this example, /dev/fd0 is your floppy drive, and /mnt/floppy is the mount point. Now when you access /mnt/floppy, you'll actually access the files on your floppy.

Usually /dev/fd0 is your floppy drive, although some distros are configured so that /dev/floppy is the same thing as /dev/fd0. Usually your CD-ROM is configured the same way: /dev/cdrom is your CD-ROM device (or, more specifically, /dev/floppy is a symbolic link to your actual floppy drive and /dev/cdrom is a symbolic link to your CD-ROM drive).

Although many Linux distros have directories like /mnt/floppy or /floppy created by default so you can mount your floppies there, you're not forced to use these directories. You can mount your devices or partitions into any existing directory you want usint the mount command.

Usually your Linux distro is configured so that one particular directory is the default mount point for one particular device. In most distros it's /mnt/floppy or /floppy for floppies, and /mnt/cdrom or /cdrom for CD-ROMs. When this is the case, you don't need to tell mount the whole device name: just give either the device or mount point. For example, if /mnt/ floppy is the default mount point for /dev/fdo, this would mount your floppy:

```
$ mount /mnt/floppy
```

The default mount points for different devices are configured in a file called /etc/fstab. The root user can freely edit the mount points configured in that file.

In Mandriva Linux, you can just stick in your floppy or CD-ROM and immediately access the files on them without mounting them first. After you're done, you can just remove them from the drive without unmounting them first. This can be done because of a tool called automount, where it automatically mounts all the partitions and devices listed in /etc/fstab, no matter if the devices are physically there or not. This way you can access devices in Mandriva without mounting and unmounting them yourself.

Question 86: Unmounting files

How do I safely unmount then?

A: Unmounting is done with the unmount command.

When unmounting, you'll need to tell unmount what mounted device to unmount, either by telling what's the device or the mount point. For example, if /dev/fdo is mounted to /mnt/floppy, you'll unmount it with:

```
$ umount /mnt/floppy
or
$ umount /dev/fd0
```

It's not wise to remove the floppy from the floppy drive without unmounting it first. In the worst case the data you were writing to the floppy wasn't written into it yet. With CD-ROMs you can't do this: the tray won't even open if you haven't unmounted the CD first.

Question 87: fstab

What is fstab and why is it useful?

A: fstab is a configuration file that contains information of all the partitions and storage devices in your computer. The file is located under /etc, so the full path to this file is /etc/fstab.

/etc/fstab contains information of where your partitions and storage devices should be mounted and how. If you can't access your Windows partition from Linux, aren't able to mount your CD or write to your floppy as a normal user, or have problems with your CD-RW, you probably have a misconfigured /etc/fstab file. You can usually fix your mounting problems by editing your fstab file.

/etc/fstab is just a plain text file, so you can open and edit it with any text editor you're familiar with. However, note that you must have the root privileges before editing fstab. So, in order to edit the file, you must either log in as root or use the su command to become root.

Everybody has a bit different /etc/fstab file because the partitions, devices and their properties are different on different systems. But the basic structure of fstab is always the same. Here's an example of the contents of /etc/fstab:

```
/dev/hda2      /              ext2    defaults              1 1
/dev/hdb1      /home          ext2    defaults              1 2
/dev/cdrom     /media/cdrom   auto    ro,noauto,user,exec   0 0
/dev/fd0       /media/floppy  auto    rw,noauto,user,sync   0 0
proc           /proc          proc    defaults              0 0
/dev/hda1      swap           swap    pri=42                0 0
```

Every line (or row) contains the information of one device or partition. The first column contains the device name, the second one its mount point, third its filesystem type, fourth the mount options, fifth (a number) dump options, and sixth (another number) filesystem check options.

The first and second columns should be pretty straightforward. They tell the mount command exactly the same things that you tell mount when you mount stuff manually: what is the device or partition and what is the mount point. The mount point specified for a device in /etc/fstab is its default mount point. That is the directory where the device will be mounted if you don't specify any other mount point when mounting the device.

Most Linux distros create special directories for mount points. Most distros create them under /mnt. If you type the following command:

```
$ mount /dev/fd0
```

Your floppy will be mounted in /media/floppy, because that's the default mount point specified in /etc/fstab. If there is no entry for /dev/fdo in fstab when you issue the command above, mount gets very confused because it doesn't know where to mount the floppy.

You can freely change the default mount points listed in /etc/fstab if you're not satisfied with the defaults your distro has given you. Just make sure the mount point is a directory that already exists on your system. If not, you can simply create it.

Some partitions and devices are also automatically mounted when your Linux system boots up. For example, have a look at the example fstab above. There are lines that look like this:

```
/dev/hda2 / ext2 defaults 1 1
/dev/hdb1 /home ext2 defaults 1 2
```

These lines mean that /dev/hda2 will be mounted to / and /dev/hdb1 to /home. This is done automatically when your Linux system boots up. If it doesn't, you'll have a hard time using your Linux system because all the programs you use are in / and you wouldn't be able to run them if / wasn't mounted. The system knows where you want to mount /dev/hda2 and /dev/hdb1 by looking at the /etc/fstab file.

The third column in /etc/fstab specifies the filesystem type of the device or partition. Many different filesystems are supported but we'll take a look at the most common ones only.

Most likely your Linux partitions are Ext3. Ext2 used to be the standard filesystem for Linux, but these days, Ext3 and ReiserFS are usually the default filesystems for almost every new Linux distro. Ext3 is a newer filesystem type that differs from Ext2 in that it's journaled, meaning that if you turn the computer off without properly shutting down, you shouldn't lose any data and your system shouldn't spend ages doing filesystem checks the next time you boot up.

Your Linux partitions may very well be formatted as ReiserFS. Like Ext3, ReiserFS is a journaled filesystem, but it's much more advanced than Ext3. Many Linux distros (including SuSE) have started using ReiserFS as their default filesystem for Linux partitions.

The filesystem name is self-explanatory. The filesystem type "swap" is used in your swap partitions.

Your Windows partitions are probably either Vfat or NTFS. The 9x series (95, 98, ME) all use Vfat (more widely known as FAT32), and the NT series (NT, 2000, XP) use NTFS. In 2000 and XP you can choose the filesystem type, so 2000 and XP partitions may be formatted as Vfat, too. If you want to be able to write to your Windows partitions from Linux, I suggest formatting them as Vfat, because Linux's support for writing to NTFS partitions is a bit shabby at this moment.

The option auto simply means that the filesystem type is detected automatically. If you take a look at the example fstab above, you'll see that the floppy and CD-ROM both have "auto" as their filesystem type. Their filesystem type may vary. One floppy might be formatted for Windows and the other for Linux's Ext2. That's why it's wise to let the system automatically detect the filesystem type of media such as floppies and cdroms.

The fourth column in fstab lists all the mount options for the device or partition. For more information, check out the man page of mount.

With the auto option, the device will be mounted automatically at bootup or when you issue the mount -a command. auto is the default option. If you don't want the device to be mounted automatically, use the noauto option in /etc/fstab. With noauto, the device can be mounted only explicitly.

The user and nouser are very useful options. The user option allows normal users to mount the device, while nouser lets only the root to mount the device. nouser is the default, which is a major cause of headache for new Linux users. If you're not able to mount your cdrom, floppy, Windows partition, or something else as a normal user, add the user option into /etc/fstab.

The exec lets you execute binaries that are on that partition, while noexec doesn't let you do that. noexec might be useful for a partition that contains binaries you don't want to execute on your system or that can't even be executed on your system. This might be the case of a Windows partition. exec is the default option.

ro Mount the filesystem read-only.

rw Mount the filesystem read-write. Again, using this option might cure the headache of many new Linux users who can't write to their floppies, Windows partitions, or something else.

sync means it's done synchronously. If you look at the example fstab, you'll notice that this is the option used with the floppy. This means that when you copy a file to the floppy, the changes are physically written to the floppy at the same time you issue the copy command.

Then again, if you have the async option in /etc/fstab, input and output is done asynchronously. Now when you copy a file to the floppy, the changes may be physically written to it long time after issuing the command. This may sometimes be favorable, but can cause some malicious accidents: if you just remove the floppy without unmounting it first, the copied file may not physically exist on the floppy.

async is the default. I suggest that you sync with the floppy, especially if you're used to the way it's done in Windows and have a tendency to remove floppies before unmounting them first.

defaults uses the default options that are rw, suid, dev, exec, auto, nouser and async.

dump is a backup utility and fsck is a filesystem check utility.

The 5th column in /etc/fstab is the dump option. dmp checks it and uses the number to decide if a filesystem should be backed up. If it's zero, dump will ignore that filesystem. If you take a look at the example fstab, you'll notice that the 5th column is zero in most cases.

The 6th column is an fsck option. fsck looks at the number in the 6th column to determine in which order the filesystems should be checked. If it's zero, fsck won't check the filesystem.

Question 88: special characters in a file name

Why do some file names causes' trouble?

A: You can have weird file names on your Linux system if you want, like for example, having spaces in a file name. You can also use some strange characters in a file name like &, *, \, $, and ? . The problems start when you try to use these files names at the command line.

When you type commands at the prompt, spaces are often used for separating different commands, the command's arguments, or different files. The shell doesn't know that the bunch of text that follows your command is in fact one single file name. However, there's an easy way to tell the shell that the bunch of text is just one file name, so having spaces in a file name usually isn't a big problem.

A more difficult thing is the special characters in file names. There are some characters that have a special meaning to the bash shell. For example, * and ? are wildcards and $ means a variable. Avoid using these characters in normal file names.

If you have files with spaces or special characters in their names, you have two ways of dealing with them: quoting the file name or escaping the confusing characters.

Quoting: Put the file name in single quotes (') so spaces or special characters won't bother you anymore, for example: $ cat 'File With Spaces.txt'

Quotes are very important. If you don't use them, cat will view three different files: File, With and Spaces.txt.

Escaping the characters is another way to deal with special characters in a file name. You put a backslash (\ ) in front of the special character or space. This makes the bash shell treat the special character like a normal character. For example:

```
$ cat File\ With\ Spaces.txt
```

Or:

```
$ rm File\*.txt
```

If the file name contains the \ character, you escape it too!

```
$ rm File\\.txt
```

Or, you can also use the quotes:

```
$ rm 'File\.txt'
```

It's a matter of choice which method you will use; quoting or escaping. However, quoting doesn't always work. For example, if you want to use shell wildcards with a file that has special characters in its name, it's impossible to use quoting because that would escape the wildcards as well, so in these cases it's necessary to escape the special characters with a backslash.

Question 89: Automatic file name completion

I was told that automatic file completion is one of the most useful features of the Linux command line. How does it work?

A: Working at the Linux command line requires a lot of typing. It would get very frustrating with long commands and file names but your Tab key can make your life a lot easier.

You have to type only the beginning of a command, directory, or a file name, hit the Tab key and the shell completes the rest. For example, if you want to view a file called unDENIABLYVERYVERYLONG.FileName.txt, all you have to type is: $ less un and hit the Tab key. The rest of the file name is completed automatically.

There may be several files that start with the same letters but have different endings. How the shell behaves when you press the Tab key in this case may differ depending on the shell and how it's configured. Usually with a default bash configuration, when you've typed the first letters of a file name and hit the Tab key, the shell completes as much as it can and beeps. When you press the Tab key again, the shell shows you all the alternatives. Sometimes you'll have to hit Tab twice before it shows you the alternatives. Now you can either type the whole file name or type a couple more letters and hit Tab again.

You can complete anything: commands, program names, directories, and file names. For example, to issue the command umount /mnt/floppy, you can first type um, hit Tab, then type /mn, hit Tab, then type f, hit Tab. Automatic file name completion makes life easier.

Question 90: Shell wildcards

What are shell wildcards?

A: Wildcards are a shell feature that makes the command line much more powerful than any GUI file managers. These are special characters that allow you to select filenames that match certain patterns of characters. This helps you to select even a big group of files with typing just a few characters and in most cases it's easier than selecting the files with a mouse.

Here's a list of the most commonly used wildcards in bash:

Wildcard	Matches
*	zero or more characters
?	exactly one character
[abcde]	exactly one character listed
[a-e]	exactly one character in the given range
[!abcde]	any character that is not listed
[!a-e]	any character that is not in the given range
{debian,linux}	exactly one entire word in the options given

You can use wildcards with any command that accepts file names as arguments.

For example: Probably the * character is already familiar to you, because it's widely used in many other places and not just in Linux. The following removes every file from the current directory: $ rm *

The following command moves all the HTML files, that have the word "linux" in their names, from the working directory into a directory named dir1: $ mv *linux*.html dir1

Hence, moving multiple files can be just as simple as moving only one file.

The following displays all files that begin with d and end with .txt: $ less d*.txt

The following command removes all files whose names begin with junk, followed by exactly three characters: $ rm junk.???

With this command you list all files or directories whose names begin with hda, followed by exactly one numeral: $ ls hda[0-9]

This lists all files or directories beginning with hda, followed by exactly two numerals:
`$ ls hda[0-9][0-9]`

The following lists all files or directories whose name starts with either hd or sd, followed by any single character between a and c:
`$ ls {hd,sd}[a-c]`

This command copies all files that begin with an uppercase letter, to directory dir2:
`$ cp [A-Z]* dir2`

This deletes all files that don't end with c, e, h or g: $ rm *[!cehg]

You can use simple patterns or combine different wildcards and construct very complex patterns. Also, you can use them with any commands that accept file names as arguments.

Chapter VI: X Window System

Question 91: Windows manager

What is a windows manager? How is it different from an X
Window system and a Desktop Environment?

A: Microsoft Windows is based on a graphical user interface
(GUI for short) where you can control the applications by
pointing and clicking. Linux, just like UNIX or MS-DOS, is
completely text based and can be done without any GUI. Using
Linux as a server is an advantage because computer resources
are not wasted in running a GUI. On the other hand most home
users or ordinary users want a pretty GUI where we can use
graphical apps and point and click to.

Because Linux is text based, you run the GUI on top of it. In
UNIX the GUI is called X Window System or X for short. The X
Window System makes it possible to run graphical apps on
Linux. X is responsible for the hardware related settings as it
controls the mouse, keyboard, the monitor settings, etc. The
graphical apps themselves don't need to care for the hardware
they're running on. The apps just talk to X and tell it what they
want to display. X listens to the apps and converts the apps'
display commands into something that the graphics hardware
can display. Therefore, X makes it possible for the graphical apps
to display their interface on the screen but doesn't control the
windows where the apps are displayed.

The Linux version of X used to be XFree86, but these days, most
new distros use X.org. X.org is a fork of XFree86 that was
created because of some licensing issues. So, if you want a GUI in
Linux, you must run X.org on top of it.

Windows manager: Because X provides the place to put the
windows on but doesn't control them, you need additional
software that takes care of handling the windows. The piece of
software dealing with the windows is the window manager. The
window manager is just an X program itself, and like the other
graphical apps, it also needs the X Windows in order to work. It's
just a special piece of X software because all it does is take care of
the windows.

189

The window manager controls the way your desktop works, on how the windows look and act. It's the window manager's job to provide ways of controlling the windows, like moving, hiding, resizing, or closing them. The window manager decides what window at the moment accepts input from you and what window is on the top. The window manager also controls the ways you do these tasks: what mouse buttons you click or what keys you press in order to accomplish these window management tasks.

Different window managers have different features, but most window managers today provide a menu or menus for launching apps. Many window managers provide virtual desktops - multiple screens you can switch between pretty much the same way as you switch between windows, but instead of switching between apps only, you switch between whole desktops. Some window managers may also provide graphical configuration programs in order to make configuring them easy.

Since there are dozens of different window managers out there, you can change your desktop's look and feel completely by changing the window manager. MS Windows lets you have different desktop themes but in Linux, you can change everything.

Desktop environments: The window manager provides everything you need for controlling the windows on your desktop. However, you may want some additional features and may want the window manager to take care of the whole desktop, but providing these additional features isn't a window manager's problem. This is where you need a desktop manager or a desktop environment.

A desktop manager takes care of your whole desktop by providing and controlling additional helpful features that don't directly deal with handling the windows. For example, a desktop environment may provide you with a taskbar or many taskbars, additional menus, icons on the desktop, screen savers, and many little utility programs like a graphical file manager, search tool, text editor, and so on.

The two big players in the desktop manager field are KDE (K Desktop Environment) and GNOME (GNU Network Object Model Environment). There are a lot of differences between them, but they have one thing in common: you must use a window manager in addition to a desktop environment. A desktop environment takes care of the whole desktop, but it's still the window manager's job to control the windows. One of the biggest differences between KDE and GNOME is the way they play with window managers. KDE has its own window manager, so if you use KDE, it'll be really painful to change the window manager you use with it. However, GNOME doesn't come with its own window manager, so you can freely choose what window manager to use with it.

Question 92: Change default manager

I have just installed a new window manager. I'm booting to command line and start X manually with the start X command.

How can I make the new window manager as my default manager?

A: Changing the default window manager or desktop in Linux is not that hard. You simply need to edit a little config file with any text editor you're familiar with.

If you use the startx command for starting up the X Window System, you'll need to edit a file called .xinitrc that is located in your home directory. If the file already is there, just open it with your favorite text editor. If you want to make a backup of this file, rename it to something like .xinitrc.backup (or whatever you choose).

If you don't have such a file in your home directory, create a new file with that name. Be aware of the dot in the file name, this means that the file is a hidden file and doesn't show when you do a normal directory listing.

Now you can use your text editor for creating a new, blank .xinitrc file. Although the file may be a complicated it just contains a single line with the name of your new window manager. So, add a line like this to your file: exec windowmanager

Where windowmanager is the command that starts the window manager you want to be your default. For example, to make Window Maker your default window manager, you'd have a line like this: exec wmaker

The commands for starting some popular window managers and desktop environments are:

KDE = startkde
Gnome = gnome-session
Blackbox = blackbox

FVWM = fvwm (or, for FVWM2 it's fvwm2)
Window Maker = wmaker
IceWM = icewm

Save your changes after editing the .xinitrc file. The next time you do a startx, the new window manager will be your default.

Question 93: Change from text login to graphical login

I want to start the X Window System automatically when my Linux boots to have a graphical log-in.

How can I do this?

A: You can disable the X Window System from starting at boot up so you'll have a text login or you can boot to X Windows so you can have a graphical login in Linux by simply editing the /etc/inittab file. This works on any Linux distro.

You need to be root in order to edit this file. If you're logged in as a normal user, get the root privileges with the su command: type the command and then the root password.

```
$ su
password:
#
```

Now you can open the /etc/inittab file with your favorite text editor.

The /etc/inittab file is usually commented well, so the file itself explains what the lines in the file mean. Look for a line like this: id:3:initdefault:

The line is usually at the beginning of the /etc/inittab file, and the number doesn't necessarily have to be 3. The number in that line tells the default run level of your system. The default run level in turn specifies what processes are started when your Linux system boots up. You need to change the number that indicates your default run level in order to specify if you want to start the X Windows when your Linux system boots up.

The number of the runlevel that starts X isn't always the same in all Linux distros. That's why you'll have to read the /etc/inittab file a bit more. It explains what number and what runlevel is used for graphical and text login. If you want to boot to X

Windows, you'll choose a "full multi-user with xdm" or "full
multi-user with graphical login" or something similar. If you
want to boot to the command line, you'll choose a runlevel that
says something like "full multi-user" or "full multi-user with text
login" or "full multi-user with no graphical login" or something
alike.

In Red Hat, the runlevel for booting to X Windows is 5, and for a
text login it's 3 by default. In older SuSE's it was 2 for a text
login, and 3 for a graphical login. So, for example, if you want a
graphical login in a Red Hat based distro, you'll change

`id:3:initdefault:`

to

`id:5:initdefault:`

Check out your inittab file to see the number of the runlevel in
your distro and then replace the number in the line to indicate
the runlevel you want. Then save the changes and you're done.

If you're booting to X Windows, you'll need a display manager.
It's a graphical program that takes care of your login: it shows
you a graphical login screen, lets you type in your username and
password and starts your window manager after you've logged
in.

In most modern Linux distros you don't have to worry about this.
Usually they install a display manager by default, so all you have
to do is change the runlevel and the next time you boot your
system, it automatically starts the display manager.

However, if something goes wrong and the X Window System
doesn't start and you end up with a text login, you probably don't
have a display manager installed. Then you'll have to install and
configure one of the display managers, like the KDE display
manager kdm, Gnome display manager gdm, the xdm, etc.

If you just disabled the graphical login, you'll need to start X
manually when you want the GUI. Just type the startx command
and the X Window System starts up.

If X tries to start up but throws you back to the command line, the reason probably is that X doesn't know what window manager you wish to use. Or if X starts up just fine but you get a way different desktop than usually, you also need to tell X what window manager you want to use.

Question 94: Running multiple X sessions

Is it possible to run two or more sessions of the X Window System at the same time?

A: It's possible. You can have multiple X sessions running on different virtual terminals.

There are two ways to start the first X session: you either start the X Window System manually after logging in or X starts automatically when your Linux system boots up. If your system is configured to starts X automatically, you don't have to worry about the first X session: it's already running.

If you don't have a graphical login, you probably start X with the startx command after logging in: startx

The first X session you start runs on screen 0. It does this by default, so when you start an X session, you don't have to specifically tell it to run on screen 0. However, you can run the second X session on screen 1, the third on screen 2, and so on. This is how you tell X to run on screen 1: startx -- :1

To run X on screen 2, you'd use the command: startx -- :2, and so on.

You probably know you have several virtual terminals. On a default Linux configuration, you have command line sessions running on your first six virtual terminals. Your first X session is running on the seventh virtual terminal (screen 0). If you're running only one X session, all the terminals after terminal seven are empty.

The second X session runs in virtual terminal eight, the third session in virtual terminal nine, and so on. You switch between X screens the same way you switch between virtual terminals: Press Ctrl, Alt and the F key with the desired terminal's number.

For example, to switch from screen 0 to screen 1 (from the first X session to the second one), you'd press Ctrl + Alt + F8. To go back to the first X session, you use Ctrl + Alt + F7.

When starting multiple X sessions with startx, make sure you have a file called .xinitrc in your home directory. It's the file that controls things like what window manager is started.

Because the default screen is 0, some graphical applications may get a bit confused when using other screens. If you type an application's name at the command line of a terminal emulator, the application may run on screen 0 although you launch it from another screen. This isn't a problem, though. Many applications have a command line option for specifying the screen it runs on. For example, to run Gimp on screen 2, you'd start it with:

```
gimp --display :2
```

This is actually an advantage. You can launch the application from any X session or virtual terminal you want and send it to any X screen you like.

To have an X session with another color depth than the default one, you'd use the -depth option. For example, to run a second X session with an 8 bpp color depth, you'd type:
```
startx -- :1 -depth 8
```

As always, check out the manual page: man startx for more help and for more options.

Question 95: Move the mouse cursor with keyboard

Is there a way to use the keyboard for moving the mouse cursor in the X Window System?

A: Yes, after running X Window System, press Shift + NumLock to turn the feature on.

Move the mouse using the 1, 2, 3, 4, 6, 7, 8, and 9 keys in your number pad. Take a look at your number pad, and you'll quite quickly figure out which key moves the mouse in which direction.

Click by hitting the 5 key on your number pad. Double click by hitting it twice.

Click and hold by hitting the 0 key. To release, hit 5.

By default, hitting the 5 key will do a left click. You can select what button to click with the /, *, and - keys on your number pad:

/ Left click
* Middle click
- Right click

Note that these just select the mouse button. You still need to use 5 to click it.

Press Shift + NumLock again to turn this feature off.

Question 96: Xfree86

What is Xfree86?

A: XFree86 is an implementation of the X Window System. It was originally written for Unix-like operating systems on IBM PC compatibles and is now available for many other operating systems and platforms. It is free and open source software under the XFree86 License version 1.1. It is developed by the XFree86 Project, Inc.; the lead developer is David Dawes.

In February 2004, with version 4.4.0, The XFree86 Project adopted a license change that the Free Software Foundation considered GPL incompatible. Most Linux distributions found the potential GPL legal issues unacceptable and made plans to move to a fork from before the license change. At first there were multiple forks, but the X.Org fork soon took over as the dominant one. Most of the developers who were already annoyed at other issues in the project also moved to X.org.

XFree86 consists of client libraries used to write X applications ("clients"), and an X server responsible for the display. Clients and servers communicate via the X protocol, which allows them to run on different computers.

The XFree86 server communicates with the host operating system's kernel to drive input and output devices, with the exception of graphics cards. These are generally managed directly by XFree86, so it includes its own drivers for all graphic cards a user might have. Some cards are supported by vendors themselves via binary-only drivers.

Since version 4.0, XFree86 has supported (some) accelerated 3D graphics cards via the GLX and DRI extensions. Because the server usually needs low level access to graphics hardware, on many configurations it needs to run as the superuser, or a user with UID 0. However, on some systems and configurations it is possible to run the server as a normal user.

It is also possible to use XFree86 in a framebuffer device, which in turn uses a kernel graphics card driver.

As Linux grew in popularity, XFree86 rose with it, as the main X project with drivers for PC video cards. By the late 1990s, official X development past its best. Most technical advancement was happening in the XFree86 project. In 1999, XFree86 was sponsored onto X.Org (the official industry consortium) by various hardware companies interested in its use with Linux and its status as the most popular version of X.

Question 97: Installing over an old installation

How do I install Xfree86 4.6.0 over an old installation?

A: If you have an existing installation of X, you should make a backup copy of it before installing the new version over the top of it.

Before doing anything else, make sure the extract command is executable, and also link it to the name "gnu-tar" so that it can be used as a regular tar command:

```
chmod +x extract
rm -f gnu-tar
ln extract gnu-tar
```

The first part of the procedure is to move the old run-time config files from /usr/X11R6/lib/X11 to /etc/X11. Create /etc/X11 if it doesn't already exist. For each of the following sub-directories (app-defaults, fs, lbxproxy, proxymngr, rstart, twm, xdm, xinit, xsm, xserver) that you want to move, check that there is a sub-directory of this name in /usr/X11R6/lib/X11. Create a sub-directory of the same name under /etc/X11, then copy the files over by running:

```
./gnu-tar -C /usr/X11R6/lib/X11/subdir -c -f - . | \
./gnu-tar -C /etc/X11/subdir -v -x -p -U -f -
```

For each subdirectory that is moved, remove the one under /usr/X11R6/lib/X11 and create a symbolic link to the new location:

```
rm -fr /usr/X11R6/lib/X11/subdir
ln -s /etc/X11/subdir /usr/X11R6/lib/X11
```

For those subdirectories that didn't already exist under /usr/X11R6/lib/X11, create one under /etc/X11 and create the symbolic link to it:

```
mkdir /etc/X11/subdir
ln -s /etc/X11/subdir /usr/X11R6/lib/X11
```

Once that is done, extract the config files from the Xetc.tgz and
Xrc.tgz tarballs into a temporary directory:

```
mkdir tmpdir
./extract -C tmpdir Xetc.tgz
./extract -C tmpdir Xrc.tgz
```

Then copy each sub-directory over to the installed location:

```
./gnu-tar -C tmpdir/subdir -c -f - . | \
    ./gnu-tar -C /usr/X11R6/lib/X11/subdir -v -x -p -U -f -
```

If you have customized any config files in your old installation,
you may want to omit those sub-directories, or copy selected files
over by hand.

Once that's done, the main part of the installation can be done:

```
./extract -C /usr/X11R6 `pwd`/X[a-df-qs-uw-z]*.tgz
./extract -C /usr/X11R6 Xvfb.tgz    # If you are installing Xvfb
./extract -C /var Xvar.tgz
chmod ug-w /usr/X11R6/lib        # Make sure the permissions are OK
/sbin/ldconfig /usr/X11R6/lib    # For Linux
/sbin/ldconfig -m /usr/X11R6/lib   # For FreeBSD, NetBSD, OpenBSD
/usr/X11R6/bin/mkfontdir /usr/X11R6/lib/X11/fonts/misc
```

Question 98: XF86Config File

Where is XF86Config file used?

A: The configuration file XF86Config of the X Window System is used by the X server to set necessary configuration parameters. It is a plain text file ordered into sections and subsections. Important sections are Files, Input Device, Monitor, Modes, Screen, Device, and Server Layout.

Sections can appear in any order and there may be more than one section of each kind, for example, if you have more than one monitor, say a video projector and an on board LCD of a notebook.

The Monitor sections are for the physical displaying devices, the Screen sections are for the logical displays, so you can have two monitors displaying the same content or entirely different information.

The option "SWCursor" in the Device section for example controls whether the mouse pointer is mirrored on an external monitor or suppressed. On typical Unix like systems the file often is found in /etc/X11 and a log file is in /var/log, typically named XFree86.0.log for the last start of X and XFree86.0.log.old for the previous one.

Inappropriate editing of this file may result in a black or illegible screen or might even damage the monitor, especially if it is a CRT. If you need to change the configuration, be sure to know how to start the computer in text mode so you can undo any changes to the last working configuration.

Question 99: Configuration Files

Where can I find the configuration files in Xfree86?

A: The configuration file for XFree86 is usually located at /etc/X11/XF86Config (but sometimes also called XF86Config-4 to avoid confusing it with the XFree86 3.x.x version). Many GUIs have been created to ease the configuration, this is usually distribution dependent (e.g. Suse uses sax2, Debian uses debconf to generete it).

The configuration file is split into sections (not all sections are required and some sections can exist multiple times):

Files: The XF86Config or XF86Config-4 is located in /etc/X11 Note that new distributions now are using xorg.conf instead of XF86Config. xorg.conf is in the same location and has the same settings and style.

ServerFlags: General server configuration options;

Module: Configure which modules are loaded;

InputDevice: Configure input devices like mouse and keyboards; To get mousewheel working: Change mouse protocol to "IMPS/2". Option "ZAxisMapping" "4 5"

Device: Configure graphic devices/video cards For Example (an nVidia GeForce TwinView Setup with the proprietary drivers): Section "Device" Identifier "GeForce 4 Ti 4600" Driver "nvidia" Option "TwinView" Option "MetaModes" "1024x768, 1024x768; 800x600, 800x600" Option "SecondMonitorHorizSync" "30-70" Option "SecondMonitorVertRefresh" "50-120" Option "ConnectedMonitor" "CRT, CRT" End Section

The 'Section "Device"' and 'EndSection' are part of the Syntax
and must be present.
The Driver is what driver your card requires. The Option lines
are passed to the driver to get wanted functionality.

Monitor: Configure monitors.
Change Identifier to whatever you want (the name and model of
your monitor) but remember to change it also under "monitor"
in the screens section. Don't forget that entering the wrong
values can damage your monitor.

Modes: Define special modelines

Screen: Define viewing screens. For example:
```
Section "Screen"
     Identifier     "Default Screen"
     Device         "Generic Video Card"
     Monitor        "Generic Monitor"
     DefaultDepth   24
     SubSection "Display"
          Depth     1
          Modes     "2048x768" "1600x600"
     EndSubSection
     SubSection "Display"
          Depth     4
          Modes     "2048x768" "1600x600"
     EndSubSection
     SubSection "Display"
          Depth     8
          Modes     "2048x768" "1600x600"
     EndSubSection
     SubSection "Display"
          Depth     15
          Modes     "2048x768" "1600x600"
     EndSubSection
     SubSection "Display"
          Depth     16
          Modes     "2048x768" "1600x600"
     EndSubSection
     SubSection "Display"
          Depth     24
          Modes     "2048x768" "1600x600"
     EndSubSection
```

The Identifier, Device, and Monitor refer to the name of this section and the names of other sections in this file. The Subsections each define a color depth "Depth" and resolutions "Modes" that you want the X server to use. The DefaultDepth option tells X what color depth you want to be default.

ServerLayout: Connect all the previous sections into a layout
For example:
Section "ServerLayout"
    Identifier   "Default Layout"
    Screen   "Default Screen"
    InputDevice   "Generic Keyboard"
    InputDevice   "Configured Mouse"
    InputDevice   "Generic Mouse"

The Identifier is just like all the other identifiers. The others are the sections of the config file you want to be part of your X server.

DRI: Configure usage permissions of DRI. DRI (Direct Rendering Infrastructure) is an infrastructure which allows for hardware 3D graphics acceleration in Linux. It has been included in XFree86 4.x.

Question 100: Start X client on another system

How to Start an X Client on another display?

A: To start an X client on another system that has a running X server, use the following commands:

1. Use xhost on the server system to allow the client system use the display. If the server's IP address is 192.168.20.1, enter the command:

   ```
   $ xhost + 192.168.20.1
   ```

2. On the client system, open a telnet connection to the server system.

3. In the telnet session, start xterm in the background with the -display and -e options. For example, if the IP address of the machine running the server is 192.168.20.1 and the client program name is named clientapp, use the following command:

   ```
   $ xterm –display 192.168.20.1 –e clientapp &
   ```

Question 101: Mouse problem

I used the xf86config program to set up my mouse configuration and then started a desktop. Everything seems to work fine but my mouse cursor is stuck in the upper left corner and cannot be moved.

What steps should I make to check this problem?

A: Before using the xf86config program to set up mouse configuration, you must identify the interface type, the device name and the protocol type of your mouse.

The first thing you need to know is the interface type of the mouse you are going to use. It can be determined by looking at the connector of the mouse. The serial mouse has a D-Sub female 9- or 25-pin connector. The bus mice have either a D-Sub male 9-pin connector or a round DIN 9-pin connector. The PS/2 mouse is equipped with a small, round DIN 6-pin connector. Some mice come with adapters with which the connector can be converted to another. If you are to use such an adapter, remember that the connector at the very end of the mouse/adapter pair is what matters.

The next thing to decide is a device node to use for the given interface. For the bus and PS/2 mice, there is little choice; your OS most possibly offers just one device node each for the bus mouse and PS/2 mouse. There may be more than one serial port to which the serial mouse can be attached.

The next step is to guess the appropriate protocol type for the mouse. The X server may be able to select a protocol type for the given mouse automatically in some cases. Otherwise, the user has to choose one manually. Follow the guidelines below.

Bus mouse: The bus and InPort mice always use "BusMouse" protocol regardless of the brand of the mouse. Some OS may allow you to specify "Auto" as the protocol type for the bus mouse.

PS/2 mouse: The "PS/2" protocol should always be tried first for the PS/2 mouse regardless of the brand of the mouse. Any PS/2 mouse should work with this protocol type, although wheels and other additional features are unavailable in the X server. After verifying the mouse works with this protocol, you may choose to specify one of "xxxPS/2" protocols so that extra features are made available in the X server. However, support for these PS/2 mice assumes certain behavior of the underlying OS and may not always work as expected. Support for some PS/2 mouse models may be disabled all together for some OS platforms for this reason. Some OS may allow you to specify "Auto" as the protocol type for the PS/2 mouse and the X server will automatically adjust it.

Serial mouse: The XFree86 server supports a wide range of mice, both old and new. If your mouse is of a relatively new model, it may conform to the PnP COM device specification and the X server may be able to detect an appropriate protocol type for the mouse automatically. Specify "Auto" as the protocol type and start the X server. If the mouse is not a PnP mouse, or the X server cannot determine a suitable protocol type, the server will print the following error message and abort.

<mousename>: cannot determine the mouse protocol

If the X server generates the above error message, you need to manually specify a protocol type for your mouse. Choose one from the following list:

- GlidePoint
- IntelliMouse
- Logitech
- Microsoft
- MMHittab
- MMSeries
- MouseMan
- MouseSystems
- ThinkingMouse

When you choose, observe the following rules:

1. "Logitech" protocol is for old serial mouse models from Logitech. Modern Logitech mice use either "MouseMan" or "Microsoft" protocol.
2. Most 2-button serial mice support the "Microsoft" protocol.
3. 3-button serial mice may work with the "Mousesystems" protocol. If it doesn't, it may work instead with the "Microsoft" protocol although the third (middle) button won't function. 3-button serial mice may also work with the "Mouseman" protocol under which the third button may function as expected.
4. 3-button serial mice may have a small switch at the bottom of the mouse to choose between ``MS" and ``PC", or ``2" and ``3". ``MS" or ``2" usually mean the "Microsoft" protocol. ``PC" or ``3" will choose the "MouseSystems" protocol.
5. If the serial mouse has a roller or a wheel, it may be compatible with the "IntelliMouse" protocol.
6. If the serial mouse has a roller or a wheel and it doesn't work with the "IntelliMouse" protocol, you have to use it as a regular 2- or 3-button serial mouse.

If the "Auto" protocol is specified and the mouse seems working, but you find that not all features of the mouse is available, that is because the X server does not have native support for that model of mouse and is using a ``compatible" protocol according to PnP information.

USB mouse: If your mouse is connected to the USB port, it can either be supported by the "Auto" protocol, or by an OS-specific protocol (see below), or as a generic Human Interface Device by the "usb" protocol.

Standardized protocols: Mouse device drivers in your OS may use the standardized protocol regardless of the model or the class of the mouse. For example, SVR4 systems may support "Xqueue" protocol. In FreeBSD, the system mouse device /dev/sysmouse uses the "SysMouse" protocol.

Question 102: X server configuration

How can you change X server configuration?

A: You can change X server configuration through the following steps.

1. Linux operating system uses a Graphical User Interface (GUI) called XFree, just because it is a free version of X windows system, which was developed by X.org website members, also getting some IBM contributions. Today, X server configuration is totally automatic, so in the end of your new Linux system installation, if you are lucky, you can reboot, without having anything to do. Nevertheless, often it happens that, in spite of an installation of a lot of packages, it display a message saying that you are not able to start X server. The reason why this happens is that your monitor, or your graphic card, is not rightly detected. So you have only to update the whole installation, until to the Summary. Here, you can change your graphical interface settings but when ask, disable the automatic starting Option for X server after the reboot. This allows using your PC in text mode, so if you want to start X server, you have manually to run "startx" command.

2. If X server doesn't work yet, try with

XFdrake

It allows changing current settings with minimal ones:

Monitor:	SVGA (not interlaced) 1024 x 768
Frequency:	60 Hz
Graphic card:	VGA standard
Resolution:	640 x 480
Colors dept.:	8 bpp

You can increase these values, by degrees, but without over clocking frequency speed. It may damage your monitor. When you are ready, run XFdrake again and select to start Xfree upon booting.

Question 103: X Fonts

How do I make fonts available to X?

A: There are a number of ways fonts can be added to X. Firstly, XFree86 has a font path which is just a list of several directories or font servers where it searches for fonts. A font server is just a background process that makes fonts available to XFree86. An advantage of font servers is that they can send fonts to remote displays.

Recently, xfs (X font server) has been patched to support TrueType fonts and run as a stand-alone program. The patched version ships with RedHat and RedHat-based distributions, and is included in XFree86 4.0 and newer. xfs is actually just the standard font server that comes with XFree86. Its source code is part of the XFree86 source tree. However, distributions have recently been shipping a version that runs in stand-alone mode. The stand-alone X font server, with the TrueType support patch (the TrueType support takes place via a font server called xfsft) is probably the nicest font management solution currently available. Its advantages include:

- Support for different types of fonts, including Type 1, TrueType and bitmap.
- Makes fonts available to remote displays.
- Greatly simplifies editing the fontpath -- you can do it via the command line utility chkfontpath, as opposed to having to edit configuration files. This not only makes life easier for users, it makes packaging safer and more scriptable for packagers.

Because different distributions ship with different configurations, it is not true that one size fits all. We can split users up into three groups:

1. Your distribution ships with a stand-alone xfs and it has been patched to support TrueType. This group includes Redhat users and users of derivatives of Redhat such as Mandrake, and TurboLinux. Debian 3.0 will also include the patched xfs, currently in

testing. For this group, the wisest strategy is to install both TrueType and Type 1 fonts through xfs.

2. Some distributions ship with a stand-alone xfs package, but no TrueType support. Note that XFree86 supports TrueType as of version 4.0. This includes Debian stable ("potato"). For these users, the best thing to do is use xfs to install Type 1 fonts, and install TrueType fonts via xfstt. Debian users can seek out the TrueType Fonts in Debian mini-HOWTO for information about installing TrueType fonts in Debian.

3. If you don't have xfs then you will need to install Type 1 fonts by adding to their XFree86 font path and using xset. using xset. XFree86 3.x users should install TrueType fonts via xfstt, while XFree86 4.x users can add them to the X font path. You should install TrueType fonts via xfstt.

The font path:

XFree86 finds your fonts by searching a font path, a list of directories containing fonts. When an application requests a font, it searches through the directories in your font path one at a time until the font is found. To make fonts available requires you to set your font path. You can add a directory to your font path with the command xset fp+ directory Once you have done this; you need to ask the X server to re-scan for available fonts with the command: xset fp rehash

Since you will want these commands to run automatically, you should put them in your .xinitrc file or possibly your .Xclients or .xsession file. This depends on how you start X. It's convenient to make two of these files symlinks to the other to avoid confusion.

Another way to have the commands set automatically is edit XF86Config. For example, to add /usr/share/fonts/myfonts to the font path when X is started, edit XF86Config like this:

```
Section "Files"
    FontPath /usr/share/fonts/myfonts
EndSection
```

The advantage of editing XF86Config is that the resulting changes are system wide.

Installing Type 1 Fonts:
The easiest way to make Type 1 fonts available to X is with the help of the Type1inst utility. This is a Perl script that automatically creates the fonts.dir and fonts.scale files that you need for X to use the fonts. Simply cd to the directory, and run type1inst. cd directory type1inst

Now you need to add the fonts to your font path. If you already have the stand-alone Section 4.4 running, you do this by editing your xfs configuration file. RedHat users can just use chkfontpath. Te format is chkfontpath --add directory

Your fonts will be available to X after you restart xfs or tell it to reload by sending a SIGHUP. You may need to run xset fp rehash as well.

Your fonts should now be available to X. Now run xset fp rehash and X will be able to find the new fonts.

If you don't have the xfs package, you need to add the directory containing your new fonts to the font path, as described previously.

Adding TrueType fonts is a little more difficult because you need to have a font server that is capable of serving TrueType fonts. Two font servers that do this are xfstt and xfs.

xfstt is a TrueType font server. While it's easy to configure and quite useful, it appears that xfs is becoming more popular. The main advantage of xfs over xfstt is that it supports both Type 1 and TrueType fonts.

To set up xfstt, just download it and install it. Once you install it, you need to do the following:

1. Install fonts into the appropriate directory (read the documentation that comes with the package).
2. cd to that directory and run xfstt --sync. This causes it to look for the fonts and create the fonts.dir file.
3. Now add unix/:7100 to your font path.

Your TrueType fonts should now display and be available to applications such as GIMP and Netscape. You may want to configure it to start every time your system starts up. Check to see if there's a startup file included (if you are using RPM, you can use rpm -ql xfstt |grep init and look for the file with a name like this: /etc/rc.d/init.d/xfstt). If you don't have an init script, just put two lines in /etc/rc.local like this:

```
/usr/X11R6/bin/xfstt --sync
/usr/X11R6/bin/xfstt &
```

Some of the newer Linux distributions ship with the X font server xfs configured to run as a stand alone program. Redhat and all the Redhat based distributions use xfs with TrueType compiled in. Debian also ship xfs, but the version they ship in doesn't have built in TrueType support.

Running xfs as a stand alone server has several benefits, especially if it is compiled with TrueType support. The main advantage is that since the font server is no longer attached to the X server, it is possible to serve fonts to remote displays. Also, it is easier to modify the font path.

As a font server, xfs has its own font path. You can place the xfs font server in XFree86's font path, by adding unix/:port to the XFree86 font path. Once you do this, any font in the xfs font path automatically becomes available to XFree86.

The xfs font path is determined by the xfs configuration file, which is /etc/X11/fs/config on Redhat, and /etc/X11/xfs/config on Debian. Redhat users do not need to explicitly edit this file; they can use the chkfontpath utility. The syntax is simple: chkfontpath --add directory

Users of other distributions can edit the configuration file as follows:

```
catalogue = /usr/X11R6/lib/X11/fonts/misc:unscaled,
...
/usr/share/fonts/my_new_fonts/,
...
/usr/share/fonts/some_other_directory
# in 12 points, decipoints
default-point-size = 120
...
```

The above would add /usr/share/fonts/my_new_fonts/ to the xfs font path. Note that the last line of the list of directories doesn't have a comma at the end. For these modifications to the font path to become effective, xfs must be told to reload by running /etc/init.d/xfs reload or sending it a SIGHUP with "kill - HUP [pid]" or "killall -HUP xfs". Alternately you can just re-start xfs, though if you do that it would be a good idea to re-start your X session too.

To prepare a font for xfs, you need to follow the following steps:
1. If you don't have xfs installed, you need to install it.
2. Put the new fonts in a directory.
3. If you are installing Type 1 fonts, prepare the new directory for the server by running type1inst in the directory.
4. If you are installing TrueType fonts, (remember, not all distributions can do TrueType via xfs !), prepare the new directory for the server by running ttmkfdir -o fonts.scale mkfontdir in the directory containing your new fonts. If you created a new directory for the fonts you may need to copy fonts.scale to fonts.dir or create a symbolic link. ttmkfdir is part of the free type package.
5. Now you can add the new directory to your xfs search path. Users of Redhat-like distributions can do this with the chkfontpath utility: Other users can do this by editing their xfs configuration file.
6. if xfs is already installed on your system, you should see which port it is running on. You can do this as follows: ps ax|grep xfs
7. Then check your XFree86 font path. xset −q
If your font path includes something like unix:/port_number were port_number is the port which the server is running on, then you already have xfs set up properly. Otherwise, you should add it to your XFree86 font path. xset fp+ unix/:port_number xset fp rehash You can add it permanently by editing your .xinitrc as explained previously. To add it system wide, edit your XF86Config file (probably either /etc/X11/XF86Config, /etc/XF86Config or /usr/X11R6/lib/X11/XF86Config), by adding a line FontPath "unix:/port_number" in the Files section.

If xfs is already properly installed, then you can tell it to reload, as described above, or restart it like this: /etc/rc.d/init.d/xfs restart. After restarting xfs, it's best to restart your X-session.

Question 104: XDM

How do I log-in to a graphical terminal for Debian Linux 1.3 distribution?

A: XDM is the most common way to log in to a graphical terminal. In directory /etc/X11/xdm there are configuration files that are executed on different login phases. Xstartup (and Xstartup_0 especially for screen 0) contains commands to be run after the user has logged in (commands are run as user root).

The path that is set for users is in /etc/X11/xdm/xdm-config. There are lines:

```
DisplayManager*userPath:
 /usr/local/bin:/usr/bin:/bin:/usr/bin/X11:/usr/games
```

```
DisplayManager*systemPath:
/usr/local/sbin:/usr/local/bin:/usr/sbin:/usr/bin:/sb
in:/bin:/usr/bin/X11
```

That will be a default path for normal and root users respectively. It is very important that /usr/bin/X11 is available for X users. If X user logs in to another machine to start and X client application, he should get /usr/bin/X11 to his path even he don't seem to come directly from X terminal. After running Xstartup the XDM runs /etc/X11/Xsession that is run as the final user. Local configuration is meant to be done in /etc/environment that is sourced (included) from Xsession if available (Xsession is run with /bin/sh and thus /etc/environment must be sh file). This clashes with ssh that supposes that /etc/environment is a file that contains just lines of form VAR=VALUE.

Acknowledgements

http://en.wikipedia.org

http://linux.about.com

About FONTS: http://linux.about.com/od/howtos/l/blfont4.htm

INSTALLATION OF REDHAT BINARY PACKAGES:
http://linux.about.com/od/linux101/l/blnewbie3_5_1.htm

Working with X-windows:
http://linux.about.com/od/linux101/l/blnewbie_4_3toc.htm

Index

Printed in the United States
119907LV00001B/12/P